London's Secret Canal

First published in 2023 by Redshank Books

Copyright © Jim Lewis

The right of Jim Lewis to be identified as the author of this work has been asserted in accordance with the Copyright, Designs and Patents Act, 1988.

ISBN 978-1-912969-57-9

All rights reserved. No part of this publication may be reproduced, stored in any retrieval system or transmitted in any form or by any means, electronic, mechanical, photocopying, recording or otherwise, without the prior written permission of the copyright holder for which application should be addressed in the first instance to the publishers. No liability shall be attached to the author, the copyright holder or the publishers for loss or damage of any nature suffered as a result of reliance on the reproduction of any of the contents of this publication or any errors or omissions in its contents.

A CIP catalogue record for this book is available from The British Library

Cover and Design by Helen Taylor and Carnegie Book Production

Redshank Books
Brunel House
Volunteer Way
Faringdon
Oxfordshire
SN7 7YR

Tel: +44 (0)845 873 3837

www.libripublishing.co.uk

London's Secret Canal

The River Lee Navigation

Jim Lewis

Foreword by Sir Terry Farrell

Jim Lewis is an extraordinary man. He is a traveller in that long tradition of indefatigable British explorers, journeying intellectually into unknown yet fascinating territory. Out of the glorious and chaotic metropolis which is London, Jim has discovered in his travels and revealed through his writing one of the great wonders of London – the extraordinary history of the Lea Valley.

The Lea Valley is the place where Jim spent his working life. The places he worked, and the characters he encountered there, drew him into the fascinating history of the place and inspired him to reveal the full story. I first encountered Jim through my own research into the Lea Valley, as part of my work in place making and characterisation of the Thames Gateway. Little did I know I could spend a lifetime struggling to learn only a fraction of what Jim has discovered.

Jim is a relentless advocate for this extraordinary place. For many years, he has been campaigning to seek recognition for the significance of the Lea Valley, as part of the rich history of London. For this small part of London changed the world – a crucible of scientific discovery and industrial firsts. His earlier books tell the unique story of the region, its scientists, engineers and entrepreneurs. But most significantly, Jim has revealed how the Lea Valley was the birthplace of the post-industrial revolution – the electronic technological revolution – which arguably began in the Lea Valley with the invention of the diode valve by Professor Ambrose Fleming. This small but inspired device allowed, for the first time, the control of a stream of electrons by electronic means, paving the way for modern electronic communication around the world and across the vast expanse of space.

Given the focus on the Lea Valley with the creation of the Queen Elizabeth Olympic Park, Jim is unique in the way he has recognised the significance of the place. In this new book, Jim has been persuaded by his publisher, a part-time narrow-boater, to take an in-depth look at the River Lee Navigation and the industrial and social history of the region that grew up around it. Therefore, I urge you to journey with him through a past which is shaping the future and, in so doing, discover ways to protect our precious environment. It is people like Dr Jim Lewis who keep alive the magic of the place for present and future generations.

Sir Terry Farrell

ABOUT THE AUTHOR

Dr Jim Lewis has spent most of his career in the consumer electronics industry, apart from a three-year spell in the Royal Air Force servicing airborne and ground wireless communications equipment. When working in the Lea Valley for Thorn EMI Ferguson, he represented the company abroad on several occasions and was involved in the exchange of manufacturing technology. Currently he is a consultant to Terry Farrell & Partners on the historical development of London's Lea Valley. He is also a volunteer with social services teaching students who have learning difficulties. A freelance writer (with nineteen published books), researcher and broadcaster for his specialist subject, London's Lea Valley, he also has a genuine passion for encouraging partnership projects within the local community that, in the long term, are planned to help stimulate social and economic regeneration.

In 2012, Dr Lewis was appointed Contributory International Professor by the Clark H. Byrum School of Business, Marian University, Indianapolis for his work with students on the modern British service economy.

Dr Lewis is married with four grown-up children and lives in Lincolnshire.

ACKNOWLEDGEMENTS

The author wishes to thank the following organisations, companies, societies and individuals for their encouragement, support and advice and for supplying many of the illustrations within this book:

Alexandra Palace and Park Trust, Wood Green, London
Bruce Castle Museum, Tottenham, London
Edmonton Hundred Historical Society, Enfield, Middlesex
Enfield Archaeological Society, Enfield, Middlesex
Enfield Local Studies & Archive, Enfield Civic Centre, Silver Street, Enfield EN1 3ES (John Clark, Local Studies Officer)
Epping Forest Museum, Sun Street, Waltham Abbey, Essex
Lea Valley Growers' Association, Cheshunt, Hertfordshire
Lee Valley Regional Park Authority, Myddelton House, Enfield, Middlesex
London Borough of Haringey, Civic Centre, Haringey, London
London Borough of Newham, Town Hall Annex, Barking Road, East Ham, London
London Borough of Waltham Forest, Town Hall, Forest Road, Walthamstow, London
Markfield Beam Engine & Museum, Markfield Park, Tottenham, London
Museum of London, London Wall, London
RCHME Cambridge (National Monuments Record), Brooklands Avenue, Cambridge
River Lea Tidal Mill Trust, Bromley-by-Bow, London
Thames Water, Gainsborough House, Manor Farm Road, Reading, Berkshire
The Corporation of Trinity House, Tower Hill, London
The Greater London Record Office, Northampton Road, London
The Hackney Society, Eleanor Road, Hackney, London
The House of Lords Record Office, Westminster, London
The Institution of Civil Engineers, George Street, London
The Institution of Engineering and Technology, Savoy Place, London
The Institution of Mechanical Engineers, Birdcage Walk, London
The National Archive, Kew, Richmond, Surrey
The Olympic Legacy Development Corporation, Level 9, 5 Endeavour Square, Stratford, London E20 1JN
The Pump House Steam & Transport Museum, South Access Road, Walthamstow, London
The Science Museum, Kensington, London
The Waltham Abbey Royal Gunpowder Mills Company Ltd., Waltham Abbey, Essex
Tower Hamlets Local History Library, Bancroft Road, Tower Hamlets, London

Special Acknowledgements

I would like to pay a special acknowledgement to the following people who have gone above and beyond with their advice and for their extraordinary generosity in providing images for this book:

Richard Thomas, Historian of Rivers and Canals and keeper of the late John Boyes archive

Phil Emery, Canal and River Trust, Delamere Terrace, London W2 6ND

Louise Burton, National Waterways Museum, South Pier Road, Ellesmere Port, Cheshire CH65 4FW

I could not let the occasion pass without recording my sincere thanks to my wife, Jenny, for her superb editorial skills and outstanding patience. The author freely admits that this voluntary sacrifice on Jenny's part has comprehensively tested the cement that holds our wonderful marriage together.

CONTENTS

Foreword	iv
About the Author	vi
Acknowledgements	vii

The River Lea: A Brief Account

A Brief Introduction to the River Lee Navigation	6
From the Most Northerly Lock on the Lee Navigation, Hertford Lock, to Stanstead Lock	18
From Hardmead Lock to Broxbourne	20
From Aqueduct Lock to Ponders End Lock	22
From Picketts Lock to Bow Bridge	25
From Three Mills to Limehouse Lock	28
The New River	30

Lea Valley Wildlife Habitats

Amwell Nature Reserve	34
Rye Meads	36
Stanstead Innings	37
Glen Faba	38
Admirals Walk Lake	40
Nazeing Meads	43
Silvermeade	41
Broxbourne Old Mill and Meadows	43
Rusheymead	43
Fishers Green	44
Goosefield	46
Holyfield Lake	48
Hall Marsh Scrape	48
Lee Valley Park Farms	50
West Side Gravel Pits	50
Cornmill Meadows and Tree Park	51
Sewardstone Marsh	53
Rammey Marsh	54
Ponders End Lake	56
Chingford Reservoirs	56
Tottenham Marshes	57
Walthamstow Marshes	59

Waterworks Nature Reserve	61
Middlesex Filter Beds	63
Bow Creek Ecology Park	65
East India Dock Basin	66

THE RIVER LEA: A BRIEF ACCOUNT

Forgive me for stating the obvious, but the River Lea was in existence long before the creation of the Lee Navigation. As the Navigation is the focus of this book, I hope that this waterway will not mind if we first give a brief account of the history of its parent.

The River Lea rises on Leagrave Common, north of Luton, Bedfordshire, from several small springs that feebly force their way through the chalk of the Chiltern Hills. This small sample of the Lea's first water has previously been trapped in underground aquifers for thousands, or perhaps millions, of years. At the beginning of its fifty-eight-mile (98km) journey to the River Thames, this trickle (depending on season) slowly meanders in a shallow channel across marshy ground skirting Wauld's Bank, a 4,000-year-old Neolithic henge, before being joined by its first tributary, Houghton Brook. The River Lea, more of a stream at this stage, leaves its rural beginnings and makes its way across the Icknield Way, an ancient trackway that runs 105 miles (169km) from the Ivinghoe Beacon, Buckinghamshire to the west and Thetford, Norfolk to the east. The stream then makes its way beside the main road, passing lines of houses, before entering the lakes in Wardown Park. On leaving the park, the water is taken below Luton in a culvert, exiting the other side of the town close to the Vauxhall motor factory. The factory came here in March 1905, taking over from the straw-hat industry as Luton's major employer.

Onward the River Lea continues until it reaches the grounds of Luton Hoo, where it becomes a lake that forms part of the estate's landscaped gardens, which surround the house. The parkland and walled garden of Luton Hoo were designed by the famous landscape gardener Lancelot 'Capability' Brown. In 1763, Brown received his commission from the then resident, John Stewart, third Earl of Bute, who became prime minister for a short time (1762–1763) during the reign of George III. Bute holds the distinction of being the first PM to have come from Scotland.

During the Second World War, trials of the now-famous Churchill tank, designed and manufactured by Vauxhall Motors in Luton, were carried out within the grounds of Luton Hoo. Perhaps not quite what Brown had planned for his iconic landscape.

(far left) Winston Churchill inspecting a tank, named after him and manufactured by Vauxhall Motors, in the grounds of Luton Hoo.

(left) An old image of Luton Hoo.

Leaving Luton Hoo behind, the river passes the sites of ancient mills. Then I imagine the Lea holding its breath as it quickly slips past a sewage works, before crossing the county boundary from Bedfordshire into Hertfordshire at East Hyde. Onward the river flows, through the grounds of Hyde Mill Farm, where the owners have restored the nineteenth-century mill and sensitively converted the farmhouse and outbuildings into bed-and-breakfast accommodation. The river carries on through the rather large village of Harpenden as it begins its turn eastwards, skirting the edge of Wheathampstead, a much smaller village with an interesting early history. Devil's Dyke, a massive earthwork on the eastern edge of the village, is thought to have been constructed in the latter part of the Iron Age (50–100 BC) and was investigated by the famous archaeologist Sir Mortimer Wheeler in the years 1932 to 1933. Another earthwork feature known as 'The Moat' or 'The Slad' runs parallel some 500 metres to the east of the site; this, Wheeler suggested, formed the principal defences of an 'oppidum' or 'tribal centre'. It is thought the 'centre' may have been the headquarters of

(below left) Devil's Dyke, an early Iron Age fortification in Hertfordshire.

(below) Palladian bridge in the grounds of Brocket Hall.

the British king, or tribal chieftain, Cassivellaunus, and could have been the place of his defeat in 54 BC by Julius Caesar.

On leaving the village the river turns southward and passes through the grounds of Brocket Hall, now a golf and country club licensed for civil weddings but once the home of William Lamb, the second Viscount Melbourne, prime minister (1835–1841). When Victoria came to the throne in 1837 Melbourne became the Queen's first prime minister and her confidant. In 1981, the third Lord Brocket turned the house into a conference centre which hosted several government summits. These were attended by presidents Mikhail Gorbachev, Ronald Reagan and George Bush (senior).

As the river leaves the grounds of Brocket Hall, part of the water forms the race for Lemsford Mill, built in 1863. The mill is now the headquarters of a holiday company, Ramblers Holidays. In 2005, Ramblers commissioned Hydrowatt, a German engineering company, to provide an eco-friendly energy source to power the mill building, which had been converted into office space. A special breast-shot wheel was designed to replace the original wooden waterwheel. A drive shaft couples the new wheel to the necessary set of gearing to drive an electric generator. This River-Lea-powered electricity-generating system was the first of its kind to be installed in Britain and can provide sufficient energy for the whole building. Surplus energy is sold to the national electricity providers.

For many years historians and others have suggested that Lemsford Mill was the inspiration for the old music-hall song 'There's an Old Mill by the Stream – Nellie Dean', allegedly written by J.P. Skelly when he stayed at Brocket Hall. However, subsequent research suggests that the song was the work of the American songwriter Harry Armstrong in 1905. The song became a favourite with theatre goers in the early twentieth century and was made popular by the British music-hall artist Gertie Gitana, whose name is immortalised in the Cockney rhyming slang for banana.

After receiving a little more water as it passes Lemsford springs, the river skirts the south-western perimeter of Welwyn Garden City and fills the two man-made lakes in Stanborough Park, opened in 1970 to provide recreational facilities for the nearby town. Welwyn Garden City was fashioned by the visionary creator of the garden-city movement, Sir Ebenezer Howard OBE. This was the second of Howard's developments, the first being Letchworth Garden City. Howard held the utopian view that people should have the opportunity to live harmoniously with nature; something that we are just beginning to understand today. For a man born in January 1850, this was really futuristic thinking.

From Stanborough Lakes, the river makes its way to Mill Green Mill, Hatfield, a fully restored working eighteenth-century watermill that is managed by Welwyn and Hatfield Council. The mill grinds organic flour which the resident miller supplies to local bakeries. Visitors to the mill can also buy small bags of the product. A museum of local history and art is located in the miller's house.

On leaving the mill, the tail stream joins the River Lea as it passes under the Hertford Road and enters the wooded grounds of Hatfield House. Here the river enters a linear lake called the Broadwater that takes the water in an easterly direction past the now derelict Cecil Saw Mill before exiting the estate. Hatfield House was built in 1611 for Robert Cecil, the first Earl of Salisbury and a trusted chief minister of King James I. Within the grounds of Hatfield House stands part of the old wing of the royal palace of Hatfield built in 1497. In the reign of King Henry VIII the palace was acquired by the monarch from the Bishops of Ely and this is where his children King Edward VI and Queen Elizabeth I spent their formative years.

In 1916, during the Great War, the fourth Marquess of Salisbury, James Herbert Gascoyne Cecil, gave over the grounds of Hatfield House to the military to allow trials of the world's first fighting tank to take place. Before the vehicles arrived, the estate was turned into a mini-Western Front, with craters, barbed wire and trenches to make the trials authentic.

Of course, the town of Hatfield also has other historic connections. In the early 1930s, Captain Sir Geoffrey de Havilland built a new aircraft factory in the town, where many famous aircraft were subsequently made. These included the Second World War Mosquito, known as the 'Wooden Wonder', and also the post-war Comet, the world's first passenger jet airliner, which flew in British Overseas Airways Corporation (BOAC) and other airline colours.

De Havilland airfield, Hatfield, factory gate, c. 1930s. Now the site of the University of Hertfordshire.

The site where the factory once stood is now the de Havilland Campus of the University of Hertfordshire.

When leaving the grounds of Hatfield House, the river continues on an easterly cross-country route until it reaches the county town of Hertford. Interestingly, the county of Hertfordshire is represented by the heraldic symbol of two rampant harts (male deer) supporting a shield with blue wavy lines on a white background representing water. Therefore, the town of Hertford could have derived its name from harts or a hart fording the River Lea. Hertford is steeped in history which cannot be fully explored here in a few short paragraphs, but I shall give a few examples to whet the appetite of the reader.

The world's first passenger-carrying jet airliner, the De Havilland Comet, in flight.

In AD 673, the first national Church Synod gathered in what is now the grounds of Hertford Castle. Theodore of Tarsus, the eighth Archbishop of Canterbury, appointed by the Pope, united the Celtic christians of the north with the church of the south. A large stone block within the grounds of the castle records the event. It is claimed that Edward the Elder, King Alfred's son, had wooden fortifications built at Hertford. After the conquest of Britain, a substantial castle was built by the Normans with stone walls and a motte (mound). In the mid-1600s, during the plague years, Parliament met at Hertford Castle.

A BRIEF INTRODUCTION TO THE RIVER LEE NAVIGATION

The Lee Navigation begins its journey to the River Thames from the south side of Hertford where originally the first of eighteen pound locks were constructed (with later additions near the Olympic Park, we now have twenty-one). John Smeaton and Thomas Yeomans (both civil engineers) had proposed, in a report of 1776, that this particular section of the River Lea would be suitable for conversion to a navigation after having meanders and flash locks removed; the latter would be replaced by pound locks. (Pound locks are controlled by gates at either end, whereas flash locks normally have a single gate that is lifted to release the water.) Now the waterway could bring shipments of grain and malt to the Capital in greater quantities and at a swifter pace than had been experienced before, when the main means of transport had been wagon and horses.

On reaching the northern outskirts of Ware, the River Lea has to contribute some of its water to re-charge the New River, first dug between 1609 and 1613 to take clean drinking water from the Chadwell and Amwell springs to supply London. By the middle of the nineteenth century, the water from the springs, which had a tendency to dry up in summertime, was insufficient to quench the needs of a growing London population so it became necessary

Hertford Lock, the most northerly on the Lee Navigation.

The New River Gauge building, housing a device to control the amount of water abstracted from the River Lea to re-charge the New River.

to construct a system that would abstract just enough water for the Capital without hindering the traffic on the Navigation or the work of the down-stream millers. The New Gauge was a building constructed in 1856 which contains what is effectively a very large ball-cock-type mechanism to take on this particular task. (There is more about how this was achieved in the New River chapter.)

It is believed that the town of Ware took its name from the Saxon word for weirs. In Roman times, Ware was an important inland port. In the eighteenth and nineteenth centuries, the town became famous for its many maltings, which kept the brewing industry supplied with an essential product. Now the town's major employer is Glaxo Smith Klein, the internationally famous pharmaceutical company. According to the Anglo-Saxon Chronicle (written between the ninth and tenth centuries), we are told that in AD 894 a large Viking fleet sailed up the Thames and then up the River Lea to a point twenty-miles from London, where a fortified camp was built with ditches and ramparts. That would have put the invaders fairly close to Ware (see more about this later).

Summer houses for the rich: Ware's eighteenth-century gazebos.

As the Navigation leaves the town, it passes, on the east side, the last few remaining eighteenth-century gazebos, which were summerhouses of the rich. Continuing southwards, the Navigation reaches Rye House just before being joined by the River Stort Navigation that now accompanies the waterway on its journey to the Thames. Apart from Rye House being famous for the Rye House Plot of 1683, there is a more recent story to be told. In 1936, during the speedway craze, Rye House established a motorcycle speedway club which supported two teams, the Rockets and the Cobras. However, an even more recent story connected with speed is that of Lewis Hamilton. In 1993, after being bought a go-kart by his father, the eight-year-old Lewis began his racing career at Rye House Kart Track and has now become one of the world's top Formula One racing drivers.

After leaving Rye House, the River Lea and the Lee Navigation pass through an area of the Lee Valley Regional Park's wettest landscape. Consulting a map, it will be noticed that the area is populated with ponds and lakes. These are not natural features but were man-made by the extraction of gravel that occurred just north of the Essex town of Waltham Abbey – famed for explosive making, propellant research and much more. In 2012, the town welcomed top Olympic athletes who were competing at the nearby Lee Valley White Water Centre.

As it journeys further down-stream from Waltham Abbey, the Navigation leaves behind the county of Hertfordshire to the west and

Royal Gunpowder Mills, Waltham Abbey, now a popular visitor attraction.

now defines the old boundaries of Essex to the east and Middlesex to the west as it begins to enter what was once the industrial powerhouse of Greater London. Reaching Enfield Lock, the Navigation passes the cottages in Government Row which provided accommodation for the workmen and their families at the Royal Small Arms Factory (RSAF), the former home of the Lee–Enfield rifle. After the factory closed in 1987, the site eventually became Enfield Island Village which now, with a commercial hub, supports a vibrant local community. A few hundred metres south of the former RSAF site, the River Lea supplies water, via a small man-made channel, to the

Enfield Island Village, the former site of the Royal Small Arms Factory (RSAF).

most northerly of the Lea Valley reservoir chain, the King George V, opened in March 1913 by His Majesty. The adjacent brick-built pumping station was initially fitted with a set of unique gas-operated pumps that have no piston, mechanical connection devices or flywheel. Herbert Alfred Humphrey, a gifted engineer, designed the pump and patented the system in 1906. Electric pumps are now used to transfer water from the River Lea to the reservoir.

The River Lea continues its journey southward along the east side of the King George V reservoir while the Lee Navigation continues in the same direction on the west side. At Ponders End, a headstream for Wright's Mill is taken from the Navigation and passes through a small industrial estate beside Duck Lees Lane, a place that I have often claimed as the centre of the universe! In 1904, at the former Ediswan factory, Professor Ambrose Fleming, while investigating a blackening effect within Joseph Wilson Swan's early light bulbs, accidently invented the diode valve, the world's first thermionic device. This was the first time that engineers and scientists had achieved the ability to control a stream of electrons by electronic means, which allows the present author to claim that the post-industrial revolution, the technological revolution, had its birthplace at Duck Lees Lane, Ponders End, Enfield. All the electronic equipment that we are familiar with and enjoy today – radio, television, internet, et cetera – can be traced back to Fleming's discovery of 1904 at a place that is thus the 'centre of the universe'.

Following the redundant headstream a few hundred metres south brings us to where it enters the site of Wright's Mill, whose modern equipment is now powered by electricity rather than water. Since at

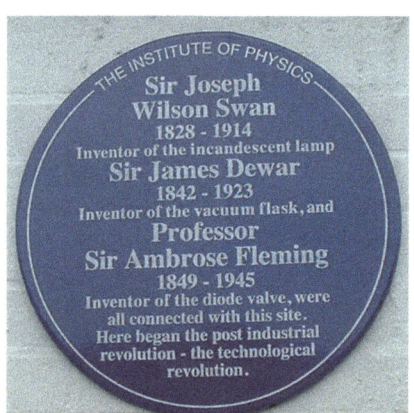

(below left) Duck Lees Lane, Ponders End, birthplace of the post-industrial revolution.

(below) Wright's Mill, Ponders End, a family-owned business.

least the Domesday Survey of 1086 there has been a mill at Ponders End. The current mill is run by the fifth and sixth generation of the Wright family and is the only commercial working flour mill in Greater London, producing and distributing a staggering range of products to more than satisfy the current popular craze for home baking, whilst also supplying a range of flours to leading bakeries.

On leaving Ponders End, the Navigation continues southward, passing the London Waste EcoPark on its west bank before flowing under the North Circular Road (A406) and then through an industrial estate that was once the home of famous furniture manufacturers and their wood yards. Onward the Navigation flows through the Tottenham Marshes towards Tottenham Locks at Ferry Lane, Tottenham Hale. Here, on the south side of Ferry Lane, the Navigation has been widened into a large turning area that was once used to accommodate the barges and lighters that brought wood from the Baltic countries to the Port of London to feed Lebus, the largest furniture factory in the world, as well as the other furniture factories that were a feature of this region of the Lea Valley. To people of a certain age, Tottenham Hale is now totally unrecognisable in comparison to what they remember from their childhood. The old one-way road system has been replaced with a new road layout and the overground and underground railway stations are now part of a new transport hub that is joined with bus station and taxi rank. A £400 million eco-friendly development with rainwater harvesting and communal rooftop gardens, by Lee Valley Estates, includes retail and office space, mixed residential accommodation, a health centre and an early learning centre. Running through the centre of the development is a linear park that complements the biodiversity of the nearby Lee Valley Regional Park.

As the Navigation leaves Tottenham Hale, it flows past Markfield Park, on its west, which is the present site of a visitor attraction: the Markfield Beam Engine and Museum. This facility is housed in a Grade II listed sewage pumping station with a popular café adjacent. On leaving Markfield Park, the Navigation is still separated from its sister waterway, the River Lea, although it will soon join with its estranged relation once again.

It will be remembered that the River Lea had its original course diverted after leaving Enfield Lock when it was given a subsidiary

Walthamstow Wetlands, Ferry Lane, developed on the site of the former East London Waterworks Company.

channel to feed the King George V reservoir. This diversion caused the River Lea to be guided around the Lea Valley's northerly series of reservoirs, eventually finding its way to the nearby Walthamstow Wetlands site, to the east of the Navigation as it passed under Ferry Lane adjacent to the Ferry Boat Inn. On leaving the Wetlands site, now joined by the Coppermill Stream, the River Lea becomes reunited with the Navigation in the area of Springfield Marina, a short distance south of Markfield Park.

The combined waterway now continues on its way through the Walthamstow Marshes, designated as a site of special scientific interest (SSSI), which supports over 400 different species of insects, plants and animals. The marsh also forms part of the former ancient Lammas Lands that were the meadows on which local parishioners had the common right to graze their animals, from Lammas Day (the Celtic Midsummer Day, 1 August) to the following hay harvest on Lady Day (old New Year's Day, 25 March). These rights date back to before the Norman Conquest of 1066 and possibly pre-date the Roman occupation. At the southern end of the marsh, a railway viaduct crosses the Navigation carrying commuter trains between Liverpool Street Station and North Chingford. (The railway was once owned by the Great Eastern Railway Company, or GER, when steam powered the engines.) Here, under the brick arches of the viaduct, Alliott Verdon Roe assembled the triplane

Plaque on the railway viaduct across the Lee Navigation, site of A.V. Roe's first flight in 1909.

he had designed before he became the first British pilot to fly in a British-built aircraft with a British engine. The engine was designed and manufactured across the Navigation in Tottenham by J.A. Prestwich (J.A.P.). Roe's first official flight was achieved on 13 July 1909 after many failed attempts to get airborne from the marsh. A plaque on the railway viaduct commemorates this historic occasion.

On leaving the marshes, the Navigation flows under Lea Bridge Road where it once provided water for the East London Waterworks Company that had filter beds and a pumping station on the east side. (The story of the East London Waterworks Company and its connections to the Walthamstow Wetlands project are told in my book *From Ice Age to Wetlands: The Lea Valley's Return to Nature*, published in 2017 by Redshank Books.) Now the site has been transformed into the Middlesex Filter Beds Nature Reserve. At this point, the River and the Navigation part company again as the River Lea takes a southward route around the east side of Hackney Marsh while the Lee Navigation continues to the west of the marsh, and for a short period becomes the Hackney Cut. Prior to the 2012 London Olympics, the River Lea joined with the Navigation again just north of Old Ford Locks, but if recent maps are consulted, it will be noted that this link no longer exists as the waterway was diverted to accommodate the site for the games.

After passing under the East Cross Route (A12), both the River Lea and the Lee Navigation enter the Queen Elizabeth Olympic Park – the River to the east and the Navigation to the west. At Hackney Wick, the Navigation, while still flowing south, is joined with the Hertford Union Canal to the west. This canal was dug in the 1820s to provide a short cut for barge traffic that allowed the boats to avoid

Lee Navigation passing through the Queen Elizabeth Olympic Park.

East London and lighten congestion in the dock area. The Hertford Union Canal now joins with the Regent's Canal, which in turn is linked to the Grand Union Canal, a connection that allows the Hertford Union Canal access to the goods-carrying canal network that links London with the industries of the Midlands and beyond.

Before the River Lea and the Lee Navigation pass separately under the road complex at Stratford known as the Bow Interchange, the River joins a waterway system called, in recent years, the Bow Back Rivers. It is believed that the first of these channels was dug in the twelfth century to help drain the area of land known as the Stratford Marsh. As commerce and industry grew, other channels were added and given appropriate names such as Pudding Mill River, City Mill River, Channelsea River, Three Mills River, Three Mills Wall River and Waterworks River. While the southward-flowing River Lea negotiates the Bow Back River system, the Navigation slips past Old Ford Locks to the west. The name Old Ford gives a clue that there was once a crossing point at this part of the waterway. When the Romans occupied Britain, they built a road that aligned with the Ford and then continued onward from Londinium (London) through Essex to their provincial capital, Camulodunum (Colchester).

The Lee Navigation combines with the River Lea (now called the Three Mills Walled River) via a short channel, behind the sluice gates of the eighteenth-century House Mill at Bromley-by-Bow. Over the years, the various rivers that made up the Bow Back River system were given different names to associate them with specific

Three Mills, Bromley-by-Bow. During the First World War, Dr Chaim Weizmann carried out experiments in the Clock Mill, formerly Nicholson's Gin Distillery, to aid the war effort.

mills or other facilities that they were feeding. When the River Lea entered the Bow Back Rivers to the north of the Three Mills site, it effectively became all the other rivers. Hopefully this explanation will allay any confusion in the mind of the reader who has troubled to consult a map of the Lower Lea Valley.

Today only two mills survive, but at the time of the Domesday Survey it is recorded that in the manors of East and West Ham there were eight mills, formerly nine. The House Mill and its partner, the nineteenth-century Clock Mill, are both tide mills that once were worked by the power of the incoming tides that were driven up the River Thames by the North Sea.

At the time of the First World War, the Clock Mill was being used by Nicholson's as a gin distillery. This is where Chaim Weizmann, who would later become the first president of the State of Israel in 1948, worked to perfect his process to distil acetone from grain. This ingredient was desperately needed in the manufacture of explosives in support of the war effort. Weizmann asked for no reward from the British government for his process, but the Minister of Munitions, Lloyd George, wished to grant him an honour. In his memoirs, Lloyd George recalls his conversation with Weizmann thus:

> I said to him; 'You have rendered great service to the State and I should like to ask the Prime Minister to recommend you to His Majesty for some honour'. He said; 'there is nothing that I want for myself'. 'But is there nothing we can do as recognition of your valuable assistance to the country'? He replied; 'Yes I would like to do something for my people'. He then explained his aspirations as to the repatriation of the Jews to the sacred land they had made famous. That was the font and origin of the famous declaration about the National Home for the Jews in Palestine.

Adjacent to the Three Mills site is the Prescott Channel, constructed in the 1930s to take flood water away from the Three Mills. In preparation for the construction of the 2012 Olympic site, a new lock and sluices were built on the Prescott Channel to allow heavy barges to move material to, and spoil from, the site. However, the £23 million facility appears to have been scarcely used.

Bow Locks with Limehouse Cut to the west.

The Lee Navigation passes the House Mill to the west and continues southward to Bow Locks, where it combines with the River Lea (which has now become Bow Creek). Just below the locks, a channel, known as the Limehouse Cut, leaves Bow Creek to the south west while the main waterway flows a short distance to complete its journey, joining the River Thames at Trinity Buoy Wharf. Here on the west bank of the River Lea is the site where the famous scientist Michael Faraday, in the mid-nineteenth century, oversaw the first experiments in the world to illuminate a

Limehouse Basin, courtesy of the Canal and River Trust.

lighthouse lantern by electricity. On the opposite bank once stood the Thames Ironworks, which built HMS *Warrior* – at its launch in 1860, the largest sea-going iron-clad warship in the world. The yard became famous for building many more ships and supplying ironwork for several bridges, tunnels and buildings. The emblem of crossed hammers of West Ham United Football Club is a graphic reminder of the club's origins.

This now completes our voyage along the River Lea and the Lee Navigation. I have tried to give glimpses of the many interesting sites that the river passes on its fifty-eight-mile journey. These are some of the footprints that history has left on the Lea Valley's landscape since its original shaping by ice sheets receding and melt-waters scouring over 10,000 years ago. Of course, there are many more places of interest that will be included when we discuss the countryside surrounding the Lee Navigation's locks.

Note

After the Romans invaded Britain in AD 43, they introduced new foodstuffs and technologies which have developed into the infrastructures and lifestyles we all enjoy today. Two of these infrastructure additions were roads and canals. The Foss Dyke that connects the City of Lincoln to the River Trent was the Romans' first canal in Britain. It was constructed for drainage and navigation purposes and is still in use today.

References

Hatts, Leigh, *The Lea Valley Walk*, Cicerone Press, Cumbria, 2001

Lewis, Jim, *London's Lea Valley: Britain's Best Kept Secret*, Phillimore & Co. Ltd., Chichester, 1999

Lewis, Jim, *London's Lea Valley: More Secrets Revealed*, Phillimore & Co. Ltd., Chichester, 2001

Lewis, Jim, Research carried out for a BBC Three Counties Radio series presented by the late Ian Pearce, 2009

From the Most Northerly Lock on the Lee Navigation, Hertford Lock, to Stanstead Lock

Beginning the journey on or along the Lee Navigation from Hertford Lock, the boater, the biker and the walker may encounter a life-changing experience as they time-travel through the region's nature and history.

Before the journey starts, it might be helpful to clear up any confusion in readers' minds regarding the spellings 'Lea' and 'Lee'. My earlier research consulted early legislation in the two River Improvement Acts of 1424 and 1420. Here the spelling was 'Ley'. In a later Act of 1571, which was intended greatly to improve part of the river as a Navigation, making the waterway a significant transport link between London and the hinterland, the spelling adopted was the 'Ryver of Lee' or the 'Ryver of Lee otherwise called Ware Ryver'. At the time, the town of Ware, which can date its history back to Roman times, was an inland port. The historian Dr Keith Fairclough, who has carried out extensive research into the history of the river for his PhD thesis, has discovered in Elizabethan documents that three spellings – 'Lea', 'Lee' and 'Ley' – were all used, although 'Lee' was the most frequent. Dr Fairclough goes on to explain:

> when discussion turns to the body of trustees first appointed in 1739, or the canalised navigation that was introduced in 1767, the spelling Lee must be adopted because that is how they were first officially spelt in the enabling acts of parliament, and because that is how they have always been spelt subsequently in official documents. Thus, it must always be the Lee Navigation, even though it could be either the River Lea or the River Lee.

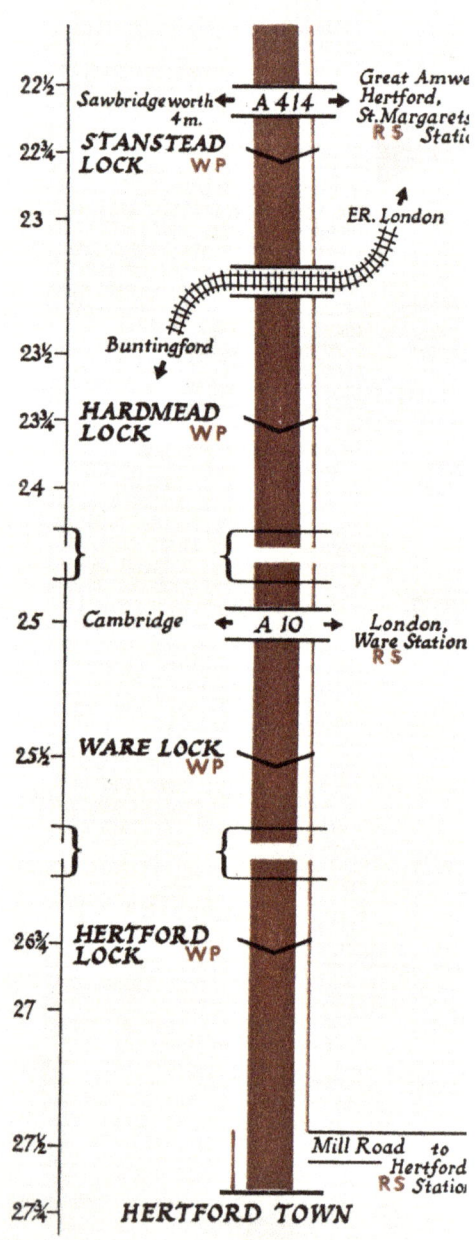

No doubt after Dr Fairclough's erudite explanation of the spelling, the reader will be requiring a stiff drink, hopefully not consumed while driving a boat or riding a bicycle along the canal towpath! My simple convention when writing is always to use 'Lee' for the Navigation and 'Lea' for the River.

Returning to what the traveller might be interested to explore on their journey along this stretch of the Navigation, they will really be spoiled for choice. Between the locks of Hertford and Ware is a mid-nineteenth-century building called the New Gauge that replaces an earlier wooden gauge. The purpose of the gauge is to regulate the flow of water from the Lee Navigation to the New River to 22.2 million gallons daily. (For more information, see the later chapter on the New River.)

Close to the Hertfordshire town of Ware is an important site that could have been where a famous battle took place between King Alfred and the Danes. It is worth remembering that the River Lea formed part of the boundary between Wessex and the Danelaw.

Since leaving industry, the author has mainly pursued a career of researching, writing, teaching and broadcasting about his specialist subject, the industrial history of London's Lea Valley. However, while researching within the region, stories often emerge that are not strictly within my subject area. I have always been puzzled by the fact that local archaeological societies, historical societies and museums have not been able to provide convincing evidence that a major battle took place in the area, when a Viking fleet sailed up the River Lea and invaded English territory.

According to the Anglo-Saxon Chronicle, in AD 894 a large Viking fleet sailed up the River Thames and then up the River Lea to a point twenty miles north of London (this would place the fleet near the town of Ware), where a fortified camp was built with ditches and ramparts. It is recorded that King Alfred deprived the Danes of escape by blocking, or possibly lowering, the river. The Danes abandoned their camp, leaving their boats behind, and escaped by sending their women and children across country to East Anglia while the men marched overland to Bridgenorth in Shropshire.

When I first wrote this story, I had not been able to discover any convincing evidence to support the account but, at the time, I explained that this should not be a reason not to continue to look. I must confess that ancient history is not within my range of expertise, but it is certainly within my realm of curiosity. As nobody appeared to have taken up the challenge to look for evidence of a site for the battle between the Danes and King Alfred of Wessex, I decided to visit the area suggested in the Chronicle to investigate. I quite quickly discovered an old earthwork, a half-ploughed-out hillfort overlooking Ware, probably Iron Age, that could have been the site described in the Chronicle. As the Danes would have needed to construct something quickly, they could have easily erected a secure fence on the existing earthwork banking. The reuse of existing fortifications by later people is a fairly common feature to find on archaeological digs. To confirm my suspicions about the site's origins, I contacted my good friend, the late writer, broadcaster and prominent archaeologist Dr Neil Faulkner, who kindly agreed to take a look. On the day of the site visit, Neil brought along a geophysics expert to walk the site with him and both agreed with my preliminary findings.

As the site crosses private land, permission from the owners was sought to put in a few investigative trenches across the earthwork banking to determine its origins. Currently, permission from the landowners is still awaited.

From Hardmead Lock to Broxbourne

A short distance after leaving the town of Ware, the Lee Navigation travels through a landscape that has been fashioned by man's voracious appetite for sand and gravel to feed the demands of the ever-hungry building and construction industry, which has paid little attention to nature and wildlife habitats. However, from the massive holes and scars left by the excavators, nature has fought back by filling the unsightly landscape with rain and spring water and creating its own wildlife haven (see chapter on Lea Valley nature reserves).

The village of Great Amwell has strong associations with the New River, the artificial waterway dug by navvies (navigators) to bring clean drinking water to the City of London (see the relevant

A BRIEF INTRODUCTION 21

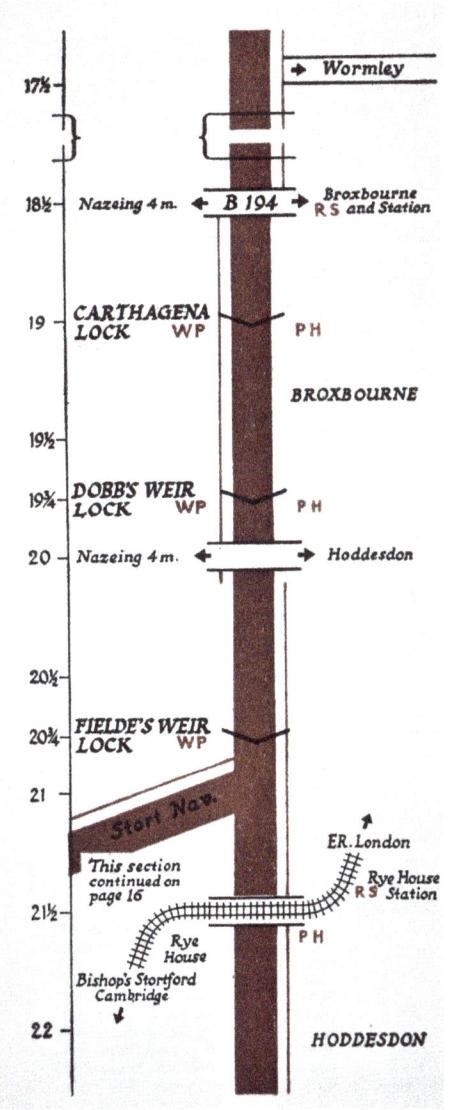

chapter for the full story). In the churchyard of St John the Baptist is the Mylne family tomb. Two members of the family were William Chadwell Mylne (1781–1863) and Robert William Mylne (1817–1890), both of whom, in their time, became chief engineers of the New River Company.

Like the nearby waterways, the whole area oozes ancient history. Below St John's church on the New River is Emma's Well, probably named after Queen Emma of Normandy, wife of King Cnut. It is thought that the 'Well' part of the name derives from a spring that Sir Hugh Myddelton used as one of the sources of water when he funded the construction of the New River in 1612.

An interesting piece of history can be discovered when visiting Broxbourne parish church, where a plaque on an inner wall describes the surveyor John Loudon McAdam as 'the great improver of British roads'. A blue plaque on Montague House in the nearby town of Hoddesdon states that McAdam lived there between 1825 and 1836. At this time, McAdam was working as Surveyor-General of Roads.

The history of the development of macadam roads began in the 1820s when the Scottish engineer John Loudon McAdam made improvements to road surfaces by using crushed stone. However, these surfaces were prone to generating dust and developing ruts. Initially, these problems were solved by John Henry Cassell, who owned a company in Millwall, London processing 'lava stone' which, with a mixture of tar and sand, was spread over the macadam surface to seal it. Further improvements to road surfacing were made in 1901 by Edgar Purnell Hooley. The story goes that one day, Hooley was walking in Denby, Derbyshire, when he came across a smooth section of road close to an ironworks. Asking locals what had happened to the surface he was told that a barrel of tar had fallen onto the road from a horse-drawn dray and someone had covered the tar with slag from the ironworks to deal with the sticky mess. In 1902, Hooley registered a patent for tarmac which was a mixture of aggregate and heated tar that could be applied to existing road surfaces by a steam roller. At the time of his discovery, Hooley was surveyor for Nottinghamshire County and he decided to try his new material on a five-mile stretch of Radcliffe Road. The experiment was so successful that this stretch of road is now famous as being the first tarmac road in the world.

From Aqueduct Lock to Ponders End Lock

The Aqueduct Lock is located in the River Lee Country Park near the village of Turnford. The only aqueduct on the Lee Navigation takes the Small River Lea (part of the old River Lea) under the Navigation. If the reader consults an Ordnance Survey map of the area (Explorer 174), it will reveal a mishmash of water channels and lakes, including Holyfield Lake, that protect the area from flooding by feeding into the River Lee Relief Channel.

Continuing south from Aqueduct Lock, we come to the town of Cheshunt. Near the bottom of Windmill Lane, almost on the Navigation, is Hertfordshire Young Mariners Base, which is associated with a world-changing event that remains largely forgotten.

On 25 June 1825, Henry Robinson Palmer attended the opening of his second monorail, at Cheshunt, built by a local craftsman, a Mr Gibbs. The front wagon, called at the time 'a transportation receptacle', had been temporarily modified to take passengers with two sets of seats facing each other. We are told the wagon was bedecked with flags and a band played, no doubt making the occasion one to remember. The year before, Palmer had designed and built his first monorail that would take goods, in suspended carriages, from the Royal Navy Victualling Yard

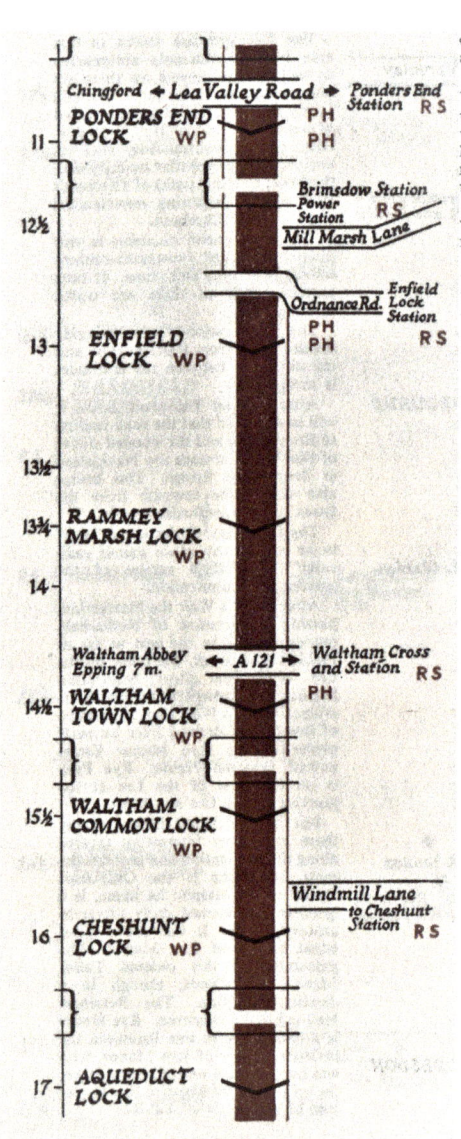

warehouses at Deptford on the River Thames to waiting dockside ships. Palmer's second monorail was a more ambitious affair than his one at Deptford, which had its suspended wagons pulled by four men over a relatively short distance. In Palmer's latest venture, the suspended wagons were pulled by a single horse and ran cross-country for nearly a mile, carrying an estimated fourteen tons of brick and lime from Rowlands brickfields, then situated north east of Water Lane. The heavy cargo travelled onward to Cheshunt Wharf, now the site of the Young Mariners Base. There, the materials were unloaded and transferred to barges on the Lee Navigation for their onward journey to building sites across the country.

Waltham Town Lock is close to the market town of Waltham Abbey, Essex, a place that is steeped deeply in history covering several periods. The church at Waltham Abbey (the Abbey Church of Waltham Holy Cross and St Lawrence), although much altered over the centuries, has several fine Norman features. These include arches, a north and south door, and a nave. Harold, Earl of Wessex, who later became the last Saxon King of England, founded the church c. 1060. After Harold's death at the Battle of Hastings in 1066, it is said that his body was brought to Waltham Abbey for burial. There is a stone slab that stands to the east of the church that marks his grave. However, historians and archaeologists have suggested that the placing of the stone may be incorrect, as Harold's body was reputedly moved on at least three occasions.

The nearby Royal Gunpowder Mills (RGPM), that once produced black powder for Nelson's navy and later cordite and other propellants used in the first and second world wars, were turned into a visitor attraction in 2001. In 1787, the mills, then belonging to the Hudson family, were taken over by the government to ensure that powder quality would become vastly improved, thus becoming one of the first industries in the UK to be nationalised. As explosive materials had to be carefully transported between the various on-site processing houses, a system of canals was dug that connected to the Lee Navigation via Powder Mill Stream for onward shipment, by sailing barge, to various arsenals on the river Thames and beyond. The site, with its many standing structures, exhibition spaces, wooded areas of special scientific interest (SSSI) and on-site café, is well worth a visit (be prepared to spend several hours).

A short distance south from Waltham Town Lock is Enfield Lock, situated adjacent to the former Royal Small Arms Factory (RSAF) and now the site of Enfield Island Village, which is run by the charity the RSA Trust. Like the Royal Gunpowder Mills, the RSAF was owned by the government and the factory and houses for the workers (Government Row) were completed in 1816. Like many government initiatives, the exercise was something of a farce as the factory had been built for the specific purpose of providing large quantities of small arms for British forces to fight the French during the Napoleonic Wars. As the eagle-eyed reader will no doubt have realised, the Napoleonic Wars ended with the battle of Waterloo, the year before the RSAF was completed. However, the RSAF eventually went on to design, manufacture and supply large quantities of small arms to the Allied Forces during both world wars and beyond. In April 1987, the government's Royal Ordnance Factories (ROFs), of which the RSAF was one, were sold to the private sector. Within months of acquiring the RSAF, British Aerospace announced that the factory would close with the subsequent loss of some 1,200 jobs. Now Britain has to equip its armed forces with small arms made abroad! Considering the delicate and somewhat nervous situation that appears to exist between major and minor world powers today, one can't help feeling extremely vulnerable.

From Ponders End Lock it is a short walk to Duck Lees Lane, Ponders End, a place which the author often claims to be the 'centre of the universe'. In the late nineteenth century, Joseph Wilson Swan, the inventor of the incandescent lamp, moved his lamp-works from the north east and set up production in an old mill building by the Lee Navigation at Ponders End, Enfield. After experiencing problems with the insides of his lamps turning black, Swan called in Professor Ambrose Fleming to investigate. Fleming experimented by introducing an extra electrode into the lamp and the measurements he made showed that atoms of carbon were migrating from the filament and adhering to the glass envelope, causing the unwanted effect. Later, Fleming realised that his experimental light bulb had other uses as it allowed scientists to control a stream of electrons by electronic means. This had never been possible before. In 1904 Fleming patented his invention, which became the world's first thermionic device, the diode valve. This massive leap in technology not only paved the way for today's multimedia electronics industry, but also created the delivery platform for space travel, email and the internet, not to mention the computer.

Interestingly, in 1888, a number of leading scientists including Sir James Dewar were called to the Ediswan electric-lamp factory in Duck Lees Lane to prepare a court case concerning infringements of the company's patent by a number of other up-and-coming lamp manufacturers. At the time, Dewar had perfected a method to produce liquid oxygen in quantity but he had problems storing the liquefied gas at its normal temperature of 182 degrees Celsius, as it was inclined to boil away rapidly if kept in an open vessel. It would appear that Dewar discussed his problems with Fleming, who had been working at the Ediswan factory on the incandescent-lamp blackening effect, giving him knowledge of pumping a vacuum and also glass blowing. It has been recorded that Dewar handed Fleming a sketch of a double-walled glass vessel that could be useful for storing liquid oxygen. Fleming got the laboratories at the Ediswan factory to produce what became known as the 'Dewar Vessel', more familiarly known today by the brand name 'Thermos Flask'. Therefore, it can confidently be claimed that Duck Lees Lane, Ponders End, residing in London's Lea Valley, which includes many other industrial sites that produced now-famous world firsts, is the birthplace of the post-industrial revolution, the technological revolution.

From Picketts Lock to Bow Bridge

Over the years, the area surrounding Picketts Lock has transformed into a series of world-class sporting and leisure facilities known as the Lee Valley Leisure Complex, the initiative of the Lee Valley Regional Park Authority (LVRPA). Here the visitor can enjoy the excellent facilities of an athletics centre, swimming pool, indoor bowls, squash courts, sports hall, golf club, gymnasium, weight training, judo room, spectator lounge, sauna, bar and cafeteria. Also within the complex there is a multiplex cinema and restaurant. The complex is well served by public transport, allowing Londoners and visitors to the Capital easy access to the facilities.

After passing through Tottenham Lock and going under Ferry Lane (A505), the Lee Navigation enters a wide waterway that was once used as a barge turning circle serving the works of the former

Harris Lebus company, once the largest furniture factory in the world, located on either side of Ferry Lane. A few hundred metres east of this part of the Lee Navigation is the must-visit site of Walthamstow Wetlands, an area dedicated to the preservation and encouragement of nature and wildlife.

In 2017, the Walthamstow Wetlands project, a site of special scientific interest (SSSI), was officially opened, gifting the British public with one of the largest urban wetland nature reserves in Europe. Funding for the project came from a number of sources: £4.47 million from the Heritage Lottery Fund, £0.75 million from the Greater London Authority and £1.84 million from Thames Water, the site owners. There was further good news when the Greater London Authority agreed to fund the development of a Wetlands-to-Wetlands greenway by improving the three-kilometre cycle link between Woodbury Wetlands (near Manor House, Haringey) and the Walthamstow Wetlands site. The cycleway is designed to encourage visitors to explore both sites, which can easily be achieved in a single day by non-polluting transport.

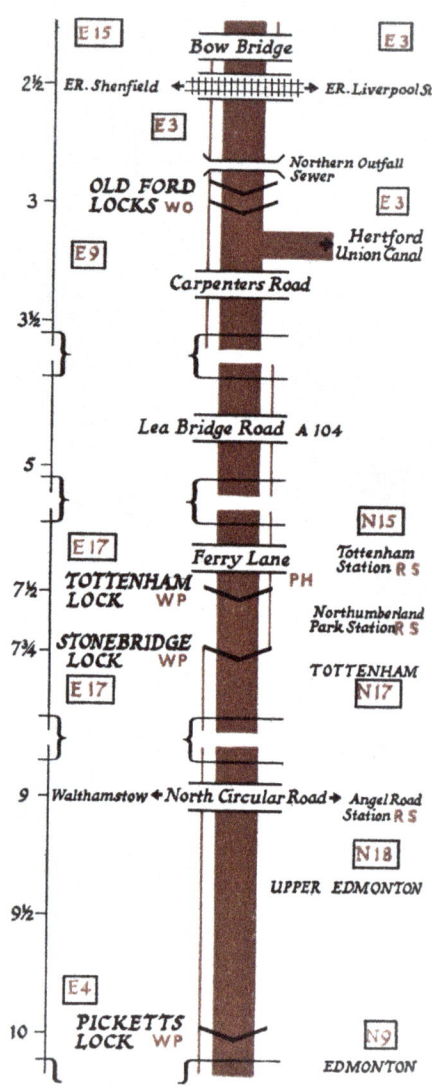

The on-site Marine Engine House, formerly called the Ferry Lane Pumping Station, got its name when the original steam engine was replaced by a powerful and more efficient ship's engine. This locally listed pumping station has been transformed into a visitor centre with exhibition space, café and viewing terrace. Educational facilities for schools and community are provided to enhance our knowledge and also encourage us to become protectors and conservers of nature rather than being uncaring bystanders.

The beautiful Italianate Coppermill pumping station, located to the south-east of the Wetlands project site, formerly used as a storeroom for Thames Water equipment, has been adapted as a viewing platform, allowing visitors spectacular views across the wetlands and the marshes.

Interestingly, before the Walthamstow Wetlands project was completed, the site was home to a whole range of breeding birds and wintering wildfowl including gadwall, pochards and shovelers. The site also has breeding populations of cormorants, grey herons, little egrets, tufted duck, coot, moorhen and other waterfowl. Wading birds like little stint, golden plovers, whimbrel, wood sandpipers, oystercatcher, snipe, ruff, curlews, ringed and little ringed plovers, lapwings, redshanks, dunlin, and green and common sandpipers are attracted to the site and will often take the opportunity to stop and take a break to feed and refresh on their long-distance journeys. In the long term, it is hoped that the extra facilities created for wildlife at the Walthamstow Wetlands will encourage some of these bird species to over-winter here. It might also be possible to encourage some of the offspring of the elusive northern Lea Valley bitterns to take up residence in the newly created reed beds on the Ferry Lane site.

The Walthamstow Wetlands project is being delivered by the London Wildlife Trust, which manages the day-to-day running of the site in partnership with the London Borough of Waltham Forest and Thames Water. Since opening, the Wetlands have received multiple visits from schools, colleges, universities, community groups and members of the public.

Continuing south from Tottenham Lock, the Navigation passes under Lea Bridge Road (A104) and shortly afterwards the River Lea splits from the Navigation, skirting Hackney Marsh to the south east. If the traveller studies recent OS maps it will be noted that the River Lea joins with the Bow Back Rivers after passing through the Queen Elizabeth Olympic Park before re-joining the Navigation again near the Bow Interchange. Prior to this, the River Lea has divided around the site of the Olympic Stadium and part has joined the Navigation below Old Ford Locks.

Just north of Old Ford Locks, the Hertford Union Canal runs west from the Lee Navigation to join the Regent's Canal. The Hertford Union Canal, known locally as Duckett's Cut after Sir George Duckett, its financier, was completed in 1830. The canal was specifically built as a bypass to help eliminate congestion on the semi-tidal part of the Lee Navigation between Old Ford and Limehouse. The idea was to allow barge traffic that needed to join the Regent's Canal and then connect with the Grand Union Canal to avoid passing through the Limehouse Basin. Now the passage of goods from London and the hinterlands could proceed smoothly to the Midlands and beyond. Another piece of early problem-solving genius and engineering.

Before the traveller reaches Bow Locks it is worth making a visit to Three Mills at Bromley-by-Bow, the site of the former Nicholson's gin distillery in the tidal Clock Mill, now 3 Mills Studios, where the biochemist Dr Chaim Weizmann, who would become the first president of Israel in 1948, perfected his ideas for the mass-production of acetone, a solvent used in the making of cordite, a smokeless explosive made from gun cotton which was manufactured in great quantity for the Allied Forces in the First World War. (For more information, see the chapter 'A Brief Introduction to the River Lee Navigation' above.)

From Three Mills to Limehouse Lock

Limehouse, now a district in the London Borough of Tower Hamlets, takes its name from lime kilns that were located in the area from the fourteenth century. The kilns were used to burn limestone (calcium carbonate) brought up the River Thames from Kent to produce lime for London's growing building industry.

After passing through Limehouse Lock the traveller will enter Limehouse Basin. This is an important body of water first dug in 1820 and considerably changed and modified in the following years, providing an essential link for commercial traffic and connecting the River Thames with the English canal system.

The area around Limehouse Basin is brimming with historical stories. In July 1840 the London

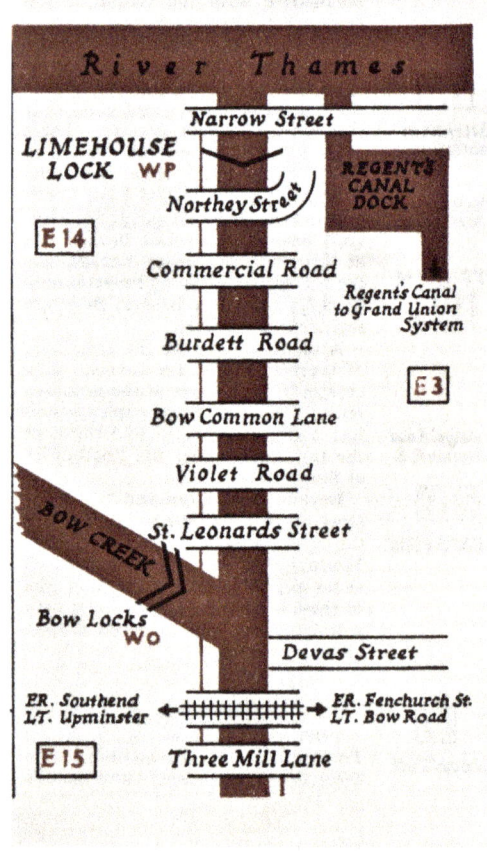

and Blackwall Railway opened a single line from the Minories, in the City of London, to its terminus on Brunswick Wharf. A second line was completed in August that year. The following year, the western terminus at Fenchurch Street was completed. At the time, there were concerns that steam railway engines running on an elevated track near wooden sailing ships in the docks presented a fire hazard, with flying sparks from the engine. George Stephenson (of *Rocket* fame) came up with the idea that the passenger coaches should be hauled by a cable attached to stationary steam engines positioned at opposite ends of the line.

Interestingly, the Docklands Light Railway (DLR) follows the elevated route of the London and Blackwall Railway using part of the original viaduct. Close to Limehouse Basin is the nineteenth-century Limehouse hydraulic accumulator tower, built to work locks and dock machinery. Another interesting fact is that after the First World War, twenty-five German submarines were towed into Limehouse Basin where they were broken-up for scrap.

Note

The author has tried to ensure that when showing images of maps relating to the various locks on the Lee Navigation, they are accompanied by stories of what the traveller might see or experience nearby. For convenience of book layout, the stories have had to be limited in number and the reader is advised to refer to the earlier chapters 'The River Lea: A Brief Account' and 'A Brief Introduction to the River Lee Navigation' to experience other nearby attractions for the lock in question.

THE NEW RIVER

An imaginative scheme to bring fresh drinking water to the City of London from the springs situated north of the metropolis at Amwell and Chadwell in Hertfordshire, a distance of approximately twenty miles, began on 21 April 1609. After several Acts of Parliament concerned with bringing water to London and a rather dilatory approach to such schemes by the Corporation, the high cost seemingly slowing progress, a proposal put forward by Hugh Myddleton (later Sir) to fund and manage the venture was accepted formally (and perhaps enthusiastically) on 28 March 1609.

Myddleton was born at Galch Hill near Denbigh, in or about the year 1555. He came from a large family of nine brothers and seven sisters. His father Richard, who had been governor of Denbigh Castle, died in 1575. His mother Jane had departed this life some ten years earlier in 1565. Hugh started his working career apprenticed to the Goldsmiths' Company and it would seem that part of his employment included banking and money-changing. Between the years 1603 and 1628, he had been returned as Member of Parliament for the Borough of Denbigh on six occasions. It is probably fair to say that, had Hugh lived today, he would be labelled a venture capitalist and risk taker.

The plan for the construction of the New River, as it became known, was to follow closely the hundred-foot contour along the western slopes of the Lea Valley, the destination being a storage pond or reservoir which was to be dug at Islington. By deciding on this route for the river, the distance the water had to travel was effectively doubled, from twenty to almost forty miles. However, what is so staggering about this project, which must be seen in the context of the day as a considerable feat of engineering, is that the channel dug from Hertfordshire brought water to the City of London by gravity only. The average fall of water to Islington was only 5.5 inches (14cm) per mile. In Britain, at that time, the use of pumps for shifting water was relatively rare.

Although construction of the New River was held up for almost two years due to disputes with landowners over the amount of compensation to be paid, the work was completed when the course was extended to Islington in April 1613. The official opening ceremony took place on 29 September that year with much celebration. When considering the problems which had to be overcome, the speed of the waterway's completion was truly remarkable. It is recorded that 157 bridges spanned the length of the river, which generally flowed north to south. However, there were also many streams to negotiate which ran west to east across the valley carrying land-drainage water. To reduce the risk of possible contamination of the clean water in the New River, these streams were allowed to follow their natural course towards the River Lea by being taken beneath the line of the new channel.

When the New River was dug, Islington was effectively a village set in open country and situated approximately 100 feet above the level of the Thames. The spot for the storage pond was quite deliberately chosen to take advantage of the natural fall of the land, which gently sloped towards the City. This made water distribution relatively easy, and it was thus possible, under gravity, to pipe water to the height of the second floor of some houses.

By today's standards water distribution was rather crude. The main conduits were positioned above ground, sometimes on trestles, and were constructed from drilled sections of elm tree trunks. Each section was joined to the next by creating a friction joint, secured with an iron ring. One end of a section was made to fit the next by shaping the mating piece like the sharpened end of a pencil. Individual house supplies were taken from the wooden main via a small-bore lead pipe which was usually terminated with a swan-necked cock for drawing off the water.

While those who benefited from this new method of water distribution were no doubt overjoyed, the system was very inefficient. Early in the nineteenth century, it was reported that there were losses from the supply of twenty-five percent attributed to leaks from pipes alone. However, it would be unwise to be too critical, considering the primitive nature of this early technology, as it has been reported in recent years that losses of water from leaking pipes in some regions of Britain have been as high as forty percent. As the population of London increased, so did the demand for fresh drinking water. Over the years, the New River saw many modifications to increase and quicken the flow into London. Bends were straightened, wells were dug, reservoirs were built and pumps installed. Today, when trying to trace the original route of the New River, it will be noticed that much has been filled in. However, due to sustained pressure from environmentally conscious community groups, a considerable amount of this ancient waterway has been saved.

Today, some of the remaining sections of the New River form an integral and important part of a much larger and more complex system of reservoirs, treatment works, pumping stations and filter beds stretching along much of the length of the Lea Valley. In recent years, a scheme was completed to take water from the New River to re-charge the region's depleted aquifer, effectively connecting the ancient artefact to Thames Water's state-of-the-art London Ring Main, which tunnels through clay forty metres below the metropolis. Incidentally, the depth of the Ring Main was chosen so as not to interfere with the Transport for London (TfL) underground railway system.

The New River, which used to terminate at New River Head, Rosebury Avenue, Islington, now ends effectively at the east reservoir on the site of William Chadwell Mylne's pumping station (now the Castle Climbing Centre) that stands above Stoke Newington in Green Lanes. I say 'ends effectively' with a certain amount of caution as this old lady still has an important role to play in keeping us healthy. An underground pipe connects the east reservoir to the Coppermill Stream in East London which runs through the Walthamstow Wetlands site, taking New River water to Thames Water's Coppermill Lane works and filter beds. Therefore, it can be claimed that, as well as re-charging the region's underground aquifer, the New River is directly connected to the London Ring Main.

Who could have imagined that over 400 years after completion of the New River, the citizens of London would still be deriving benefit from the water brought to them by the remarkable skill and achievements of those early engineers and surveyors who designed and planned this waterway? Also, we should not forget the contribution made by the labourers, who through hard manual toil shifted hundreds of tons of earth in digging the course of the river, no doubt helped in their endeavours by the odd horse and cart to take away the spoil.

References

Author unknown, 'London's Water Supply in the 21st Century', a strategy for water treatment and trunk distribution, published by Thames Water, February 1986

Harwood, Elain, 'The New River', Report by English Heritage, August 1989

LEA VALLEY WILDLIFE HABITATS

Those who travel along the Lee Navigation should take the opportunity to explore the range of nearby wildlife habitats that are close to the waterway. To help locate the various habitats, area postcodes for the sites have been given.

We are extremely fortunate to have the Lee Valley Regional Park Authority (LVRPA) which, with the help of recognised organisations and volunteers, has been doing its utmost to create and manage the many wildlife habitats within the region for the last fifty-odd years. These habitats, many rescued from the aftermath of sand, gravel and brick clay extraction, have encouraged the return of a diverse range of wildlife and plant species. This commitment by the LVRPA is having a major impact on the region's natural environment as it is helping many of the rarer species of flora and fauna to escape extinction's grasp.

The Lee Valley Regional Park is a twenty-six-mile linear park that extends along the valley floor from Ware, Hertfordshire in the north to the River Thames in the south. On the way southward, the park straddles the boundaries of Essex to the east and Hertfordshire and Middlesex to the west, providing a green lung for the citizens of London. There can be few capital cities around the world that can offer their citizens such a range of pleasant and healthy outdoor and indoor activities. These include the playing of various sports, walking, biking, boating and caravanning – not forgetting the opportunities for bird-watching and visiting the many museums and other visitor attractions that can be found around the region. Londoners are really spoiled for so much choice right on their doorstep.

Amwell Nature Reserve (Amwell Lane, Stanstead Abbots, Hertfordshire SG12 9SN)

The reserve, managed by the Herts and Middlesex Wildlife Trust, is the most northerly of the reserves within the LVRPA boundaries. It is also one of the last areas in the Lea Valley where gravel extraction took place. Over the past few decades, with a little help from the relevant agencies, nature has slowly claimed back much

Amwell Nature Reserve, where gravel was once extracted.

(below right) Shoveler, one of the many water birds to be seen on the Lea Valley reserves.

(below) The elusive bittern.

of its original homeland. The reserve is one of four sites within the park that together have been designated as the Lee Valley Special Protection Areas (SPAs) and which support numbers of internationally important wintering wildfowl. A patchwork of diverse habitats makes up the reserve. These include lakes, grasslands, woodlands and water courses.

Hides provide the visitor with elevated views over the reed beds and during the winter months, wildfowl such as tufted duck, pochard, gadwall and shoveler can be seen. Other winter visitors include smew and the elusive bittern. In spring, waders appear and little ringed plovers breed on site. They are regularly joined by other waders like redshank and green sandpiper, and occasionally by rarer waders such as dunlin.

During the summer months, a common tern colony takes up residence on purpose-built rafts deployed on one of the lakes, and in a small meadow marsh orchids bloom in early June. A boardwalk trail will allow the visitor to get up close and personal to nineteen species of the reserve's breeding damselflies and dragonflies. In the sky above, birds of prey including buzzard, sparrowhawk and hobby may be seen.

Rye Meads (Rye Road, Hoddesdon, Hertfordshire ST12 8JS)

Herts and Middlesex Wildlife Trust and the Royal Society for the Protection of Birds (RSPB) jointly manage this site, which is made up of flood meadows, reed beds, lakes and wet woodland and forms part of the Lea Valley Special Protection Areas.

In the summer months, a colony of common tern nests on rafts relatively close to the gadwall hide, and not far away an artificial bank has been created to attract nesting kingfishers. The activities of these colourful birds can be watched from a dedicated kingfisher hide. Nesting kestrels, long-tailed tit and reed warbler occupy the reserve during the summer.

Wildfowl such as shoveler, gadwall and tufted duck inhabit the lakes in winter, and in the wet scrape areas green sandpipers dabble for food. It is possible for a fortunate visitor to spot a bittern in the

Rye Meads Nature Reserve.

(above) A kingfisher with a catch at Rye Meads Nature Reserve.

(above right) A pair of common tern on Rye Meads Nature Reserve.

reed beds. These birds are now becoming familiar visitors to the Lea Valley reserves.

The otter, another elusive animal, which had become extinct in the region and was reintroduced to the Amwell Nature Reserve some years ago, has left 'spraints' (faeces) which show that this animal's nocturnal hunting territory now includes the reserve.

To help conserve rare plant species such as the meadow rue, konik ponies have been introduced to graze the wet meadow areas. Water buffalo were also used in the past but when the tough grazing was done, they were retired. Controlling the vegetation in this way has encouraged wading birds like the lapwing to nest.

Stanstead Innings (Marsh Lane, Stanstead Abbots, Hertfordshire SG12 8HL)

This reserve is solely managed by the Lee Valley Regional Park Authority, which has carried out extensive reed-bed improvements and also maintains a continuing programme of habitat improvement. The boardwalk provides a pleasant viewing platform and complements the shoveler hide, from which gadwall, tufted duck and shoveler may be observed. Looking from the sandpiper hide to the shallow-water areas, teal, lapwing and green sandpiper can be seen feeding in the margins. Also, visitors to the hide in winter months may be rewarded by the sight of bittern roosting in the reed beds, as these birds regularly use the site during this time of year.

Stanstead Innings Nature Reserve.

Ragged robin among other wildflowers on Stanstead Innings Nature Reserve.

Late spring brings the wildflower meadows to life and it is a joy to see the blooms of ragged robin and bee orchids lighting up the world in the early sunshine. The flowers offer a colourful welcome to the different species of warblers, which include reed and sedge.

Glen Faba (Glen Faba Road, Nazeing, Hertfordshire CM19 5EX)

This reserve consists of two lakes fringed by reed beds and is surrounded with wooded clumps and wildflower meadows. Wigeon, gadwall and tufted duck can be seen on the open water areas. Glen Faba's largest wooded island supports a small colony of

A wigeon on Glen Faba Nature Reserve.

Glen Faba Nature Reserve with power station in the background.

A little egret looking for lunch.

cormorants and is also home to a heronry. Throughout the year, little grebe may be seen on the lake called the Stort Pit. In the summer months, the surrounding reed beds provide habitats for reed and sedge warbler and also reed bunting, which frequent the site throughout the year. Take a stroll on a warm summer evening and you could witness bats performing their aerobatic manoeuvres as they search for their supper.

Glen Faba Nature Reserve.

Admirals Walk Lake (Admirals Walk, Hoddesdon, Hertfordshire EN11 8AB)

The River Lynch flows along the northern boundary of this twenty-five-acre, shallow, spring-fed lake bordered with wooded areas. This combined area of water and woods provides the perfect habitat for a variety of insects, including dragonfly and black-tailed skimmers. All may be seen during the summer months. The white-legged damselfly once frequented this site but has not been seen for some time. This could be a warning of how delicately nature is balanced!

From April to October, particularly on warm evenings, the reserve becomes the feeding ground for pipistrelle and other species of bats. The rarer species, Daubenton's bat, named after the French naturalist Louis-Jean-Marie Daubenton (1716–1800), can be seen hunting for insects as it skims close to the water. This characteristic hunting habit distinguishes it from the pipistrelles, which tend to fly higher and do not always frequent wetland habitats. Other distinguishing features of Daubenton's bat, over the pipistrelle, include the fact that the former has a reddish-pink face and nose, and no fur around the eye area.

Coot and little grebe can be seen on the open water areas throughout the year, and during the summer months the reserve becomes a popular foraging area for swallow and sand martin.

Nazeing Meads (Dobbs Weir Road, Nazeing, Essex EN9 2PD)

Here, advantage has been taken of the River Lea flood-relief system and the three large settlement lagoons now provide a welcome food source for wildlife. Diving birds including the tufted duck revel in foraging beneath the deep water. From the bridge across the flood-relief channel, wintering duck including goldeneye and goosander may be seen. Also, during winter months, there is normally a large roost of common and black-headed gulls, and on occasion the rarer Mediterranean gull might be sighted.

Nazeing Meads Nature Reserve.

Silvermeade (Mill Lane, Broxbourne, Hertfordshire EN10 6LX)

Silvermeade Nature Reserve.

This site provides the ideal habitat for the endangered water vole, an animal immortalised as Ratty in the children's book *Wind in the Willows*. In the 1920s, the North American mink was introduced to Britain and bred on special farms for its fur. Fur was a popular material, particularly in women's fashion, and by the mid-1950s several hundred fur farms were thriving in the UK. As is inevitable, some of the animals escaped and others were released by well-meaning animal rights activists who clearly had no idea what devastation their actions would wreak on the indigenous wildlife. Mink are voracious hunters and will take smallish animals, the water vole being a favourite dish of the day. They will also take birds, frogs, fish and bird eggs. However, the good news is that surveys carried out by ecologists from the Canal and River Trust have shown that our carefully managed nature reserves are helping the water voles make a comeback. At the same time, wild mink numbers must be monitored and the animal kept under control. Some naturalists have suggested that the increasing otter population might be playing a part in this.

The Silvermeade site consists of wet meadows that are crisscrossed by a series of ditches, pools and reed beds which make the area ideal for dragonflies and also the endangered water vole. With

Water vole on Silvermeade Nature Reserve.

Cuckooflower on Silvermeade Nature Reserve.

patience, this attractive creature may be viewed in spring as water voles tend to re-examine their territories around this time of year. Clues to their existence can be seen throughout the year as it is possible the visitor might spot droppings and also pathways running through the vole's neatly cropped grass and along the banks of ditches.

Spring is a good time to see the delicate pink-white cuckooflower, which blooms around the time when the bird is first heard, hence the name. Also about this time, amongst the grasses and sedge in the wet meadow areas, the ragged robin shows its beautiful pink flowers.

The earliest of the dragonflies to emerge is the hairy variety, which can be seen from May onwards hunting for food above the site's numerous

ditches. Later in the year, these dragonflies are joined by the banded demoiselle, sporting a glittering blue body; the male of the species is identified by the dark banding on the wings.

Grass snakes, which are non-venomous and the largest of our British species, are often seen hunting in the long grass along the edge of water channels. Being good swimmers, their main meals are normally amphibians – frogs, toads and newts – although they have occasionally been known to take small mammals and birds. Their natural enemies are badgers, hedgehogs, foxes and also birds of prey, although the domestic cat can be a problem to this protected species.

Broxbourne Old Mill and Meadows (Mill Lane, Broxbourne, Hertfordshire EN10 6LX)

Broxbourne Mill is first mentioned in the Domesday Book – a mill has stood on this site for over 900 years. Milling of grain ceased in 1891 and afterwards the mill had various uses until it was destroyed by fire in 1949. In the late 1970s, the Lee Valley Regional Park Authority restored the waterwheel by replacing the paddles with recycled plastic replicas. Apart from helping to reduce the cost of maintenance, the LVRPA restoration work will help to remind us and future generations of Broxbourne's industrial past.

Clumps of giant horsetail, a peculiar-looking plant that can reach around 1.5 metres (5 feet) tall, sometimes referred to as the 'living fossil', may be found here. The kingfisher and grey wagtail are regular visitors to the millstream and pool area.

Rusheymead (Mill Lane, Broxbourne, Hertfordshire EN10 6LX)

This site is a mixture of open grassland and scrub with areas of mature woodland. During the summer months, flocks of small birds are attracted to the site, probably as the scrub and woodland provide safe cover from hunting sparrowhawks. The summer is a good time to see warblers and bullfinches, which can be viewed throughout the year. On the grassy areas, green woodpeckers, a ground-feeding bird, can be seen searching for ants and their eggs, which are a favourite meal.

Fishers Green (Stubbins Hall Lane, Crooked Mile, Waltham Abbey, Essex EN9 2EF)

This site forms part of the Lee Valley Park Special Protection Area (SPA) and is the centrepiece of Lee Valley Country Park, where the Turnford and Cheshunt Pits provide an important haven for wintering wildfowl. The site's Seventy Acres Lake has seen extensive improvements to reed beds as the LVRPA wish to attract visiting bitterns to take up permanent residence and allow them to breed.

Fishers Green Nature Reserve.

A relative of the heron family, the bittern, according to the Royal Society for the Protection of Birds (RSPB), is making a comeback in the UK after almost reaching extinction. In the Middle Ages, the bird was a delicacy at banquets and later in the eighteenth and nineteenth centuries the birds' natural habitats were destroyed when polluting discharges occurred as the region became more industrialised. Also, the extraction of sand and gravel for building and civil-engineering projects destroyed reed beds and water courses. If the LVRPA habitat-regeneration programme works, then, in future springs, the booming mating call of the male bittern will be heard like a ship's foghorn across the Lea Valley. Unfortunately, during the winter months, the bittern is not easy to see, as the bird's stripy brown plumage blends perfectly with the reeds when it is hunting at the water's edge for fish and amphibians.

LEA VALLEY WILDLIFE HABITATS

A tern posing for the camera.

The elusive bittern, Fishers Green Nature Reserve.

(above left) Bittern hunting in the reeds at Fishers Green Nature Reserve.

(above right) A smew on a visit to Fishers Green Nature Reserve.

Orchids, not early marsh orchid.

Roesel's bush cricket.

Throughout the year, the reed beds provide a habitat for other birds like snipe, lapwing and also the elusive water rail. Islands on the site's lakes also attract snipe and lapwing and wintering wildfowl like gadwall, smew, shoveler, goldeneye and goosander; and on rare occasions, the pintail can be seen on the lakes. During the summer months, a common tern and black-headed gull colony takes over the rafts on Seventy Acres Lake.

In spring and early summer, particularly at dawn or dusk, the visitor might hear the beautiful song of the nightingale when strolling past the wooded area north of Fishers Green car park. Keeping a watchful eye open along Hooks Marsh Ditch, close to the Bittern Information Point, water voles may be seen going about their business. Also be on the lookout for an iridescent flash of blue above the watercourses as kingfishers are commonly seen in this area.

Goosefield (Stubbins Hall Lane, Crooked Mile, Waltham Abbey, Essex EN9 2EF)

To attract different species of bird and other wildlife to an area there is a need for a range of habitats to suit different individual hunting, nesting and feeding habits. Fortunately, the Lee Valley Regional Park Authority, with its partners, has an ongoing programme to create such places. Goosefield is a particularly good example, as the wet meadows punctuated with shallow pools and ditches provide excellent habitat for waders and grazing wildfowl. However, despite all the good intentions of the partners to develop new wildlife habitats, progress has been delayed by an unwelcome outsider.

Goosefield Nature Reserve, as seen from the hide.

New Zealand pigmyweed (*Crassula helmsii*), a non-native invasive plant from Australia and New Zealand, has been discovered on this site. The plant grows vigorously in our waterways, choking the system and out-competing native plants. This has caused the LVRPA to curtail their habitat management programme by reducing the amount of water allowed onto the site until the problem has been satisfactorily controlled. There are suggestions that the invader was first discovered in Britain in the 1970s residing in a roadside pond close to houses in the New Forest area of Hampshire and has since spread to other sites across the UK. However, further research suggests that the plant first came to Britain as early as 1911 and there are other reports of the plant being grown at an Enfield nursery in the 1920s.

The plant is easily spread by tiny fragments carried in flowing water and can also be distributed by vehicles, machinery, birds, animals and people.

While this is not a happy situation to be contemplating in the year 2023, it is certainly a wake-up call to all of us who wish to see nature returned to its former glory after man's un-thoughtful interventions. We must also be exceptionally vigilant with regard to the plants that we select for our gardens. Government agencies across the world must also ensure that effective and watertight controls are in place to prevent nurseries, garden centres, aquatic centres and unthinking people from importing any type of plant that could be harmful to their country's indigenous flora and fauna. Currently, it is an offence to allow *Crassula* to grow in the wild. However, my Lee Valley Regional Park contacts point out that 'new invasive species are arriving all the time'. This might appear to be an alarming revelation but at least it should give us a large amount of confidence that a responsible body is always watchful and is monitoring the situation on our behalf; nevertheless, this should not prevent us as individuals from being exceptionally vigilant.

Holyfield Lake (Stubbins Hall Lane, Crooked Mile, Waltham Abbey, Essex EN9 2EF)

Throughout the year, the lake is home to great crested grebe, little grebe and coot. From the path that goes towards the grebe hide the visitor will see a cormorant roost and also a heronry. When walking through the River Lee Country Park the visitor is sure to come across many clumps of alder, as the tree is prevalent in damp and boggy areas. In winter, large flocks of siskin and tit can often be seen in the upper canopy feeding on the plentiful supply of alder seeds.

Holyfield Lake Nature Reserve, picture taken from the hide.

Hall Marsh Scrape (Fishers Green Lane, Crooked Mile, Waltham Abbey, Essex EN9 2ED)

The site consists of four shallow artificial scrapes and gravel islands that have been designed to attract waders. In a world where many animals and plants are on the verge of extinction it is nice to see that organisations like the LVRPA and its partners are helping to bring about programmes for species diversification across the

Hall Marsh Scrape.

region. Here, on Hall Marsh Scrape, we see another example of the design and re-creation of lost habitats that have been destroyed through man's lack of understanding that a fragile balance exists between humans and nature. Although there are still deniers with regard to how our activities affect the climate, fortunately there is a growing scientific consensus that would suggest that reducing harmful emissions, restoring lost forests and hedgerows, and generally respecting our environment is the most sensible long-term way of protecting our planet.

In the spring, the new shingle islands provide the ideal habitat for the little ringed plover, returning from Africa to breed. Also regular visitors to the Scrape are common and green sandpipers as they pass through the valley on their long migration from Northern Europe to Africa. These waders were once residents of the region and it is hoped that by providing them with the right kind of habitat, they will be encouraged, once again, to take up permanent residence.

During the summer months, common tern can be seen overhead as they fly from their colony on Seventy Acres Lake and hobbys can also be seen hunting for their favourite food, as dragonflies dart energetically above the adjacent flood-relief channel.

In winter, the site is popular with wigeon, gadwall and shoveler, and large flocks of lapwing and occasionally golden plover can be seen. Rare sightings of pintail, spoonbill and spotted crake have been made, which suggest that the Scrape is a location worth a visit.

Lee Valley Park Farms (Stubbins Hall Lane, Crooked Mile, Waltham Abbey, Essex EN9 2EF)

There are two farms on this site, Hayes Hill Farm and Holyfield Hall Farm, each giving the visitor a different experience. Hayes Hill Farm has been designed to introduce children to a wide range of domesticated animals, including cattle, sheep, pigs, goats, rabbits, guinea pigs and chickens, and has proved to be a popular family day out for many years.

Great days out at Lee Valley Park Farms – something for the whole family.

Holyfield Hall Farm is a mixed dairy, beef and arable farm that demonstrates quite perfectly how farming and wildlife can co-exist. Field margins have been encouraged, as their variety of plants and grasses provide habitats for insects which provide food for nesting whitethroats and yellowhammers in the nearby hedgerows. Small mammals also flourish in the margins and attract kestrels, barn owls, little owls and sparrowhawks. During autumn and spring migration, wheatears can regularly be seen around the field margins, while fallow and muntjac deer are present on the farms.

West Side Gravel Pits (Windmill Lane, Cheshunt, Hertfordshire EN8 9AJ)

These water-filled gravel pits, and the grassland areas around them, located west of the Lee Navigation, provide a place where rare orchids thrive. When ash from the old coal-burning Metropolitan Power Stations, particularly those at Brimsdown, had to be got rid of, the nearby water-filled pits provided the ideal place for the waste to be dumped. At the time, nobody could have predicted, or would have given a thought to, the effect this might have on the surrounding grassland areas. It would seem that water from within the pits has allowed the ash to leach nutrients into the surrounding soil, which has accidentally encouraged the growth of a variety of orchids, particularly in the North Metropolitan and Bowyers Water areas. These include early marsh, southern marsh, common spotted, pyramidal, twayblade and bee orchids. In the summer, Bowyers Water also has a magnificent display of water lilies.

A great summer-months attraction can be seen, or perhaps more correctly heard, in the areas of Thistly and Cheshunt Marsh, at a time when grasshoppers and crickets become their most active. Listen for the characteristic hissing sound (which some have likened to electricity-pylon insulators fizzing during damp weather) of Roesel's bush cricket. The insect is named after the German miniature portrait painter and naturalist August Johann Roesel von Rosenhof (1705–1759). Also during this time of year, watch out for the different varieties of butterflies, particularly the speckled wood, which flitter regularly across woodland paths on sunny days.

Cornmill Meadows and Tree Park (Crooked Mile, Waltham Abbey, Essex EN9 2ES)

Cornmill Meadows reserve, within the River Lea floodplain.

There are few remaining examples of natural floodplain within the boundaries of the Lee Valley Regional Park, but Cornmill Meadows can claim 'semi-natural' status as it has avoided the devastating effect of the gravel extractor's machinery. The area is crisscrossed by a number of waterways, ditches and pools which attract a variety of wildlife throughout the year. Hay meadows and woodland complement the site and in the tree park there is a network of glades and paths to explore. The site is located just east of the Royal Gunpowder Mills, an attraction well worth a visit as part of the mills complex is a nature reserve in its own right. Cornmill Stream, part of the River Lea network, runs through the meadows and once powered the mill and filled the fish ponds, the remains of both of which can still be seen, within the precincts of the Abbey.

A hairy dragonfly at Cornmill Meadows.

A lapwing visits.

Over half of the dragonfly species found in the UK can be seen at this site, notably the white-legged damselfly and the hairy dragonfly. A stroll through the wooded glades on a mild evening in late summer can be particularly rewarding to view large numbers of migrant hawker dragonfly.

The spring and autumn seasons are the best times to see species like the occasional ruff and black-tailed godwit, alongside the more frequent redshank and common and green sandpiper. In winter,

A visit from a green sandpiper.

large flocks of teal and wigeon can be viewed which are often joined by even larger flocks of lapwings and occasionally golden plover. As might be expected at a dragonfly reserve, hobbys are often spotted hunting their prey.

Sewardstone Marsh (Sewardstone Road, Near Chingford, London E4 7RA)

Sewardstone Marsh is the site of the former Knight's gravel pits, which have been in-filled with water. The marsh also includes the wet grassland area of Patty Pool Mead where snipe can be seen feeding in the winter and long-eared owl have recently been spotted using the marsh at this time of year. Scrub clearance along the site's ditches has improved habitat for water vole, which may be why the long-eared owl has recently been seen.

In the summer, the beautiful song of the nightingale may be heard and, if fortunate, the visitor might catch a fleeting glimpse of this elusive bird. The nightingale is a smallish bird about the size of a house sparrow. It has a light brown back and a buff-to-white breast and underbelly. The bird tends to hide in dense scrub and woodland areas.

A snipe on Sewardstone Marsh Nature Reserve.

At the northern end of the marsh, west of the flood-relief channel, is Enfield Island Village. This is a relatively new mixed housing development with a small retail and commercial centre. The centre has been sensitively constructed around a restored and modified Grade II listed building which was once a large machine room. Rents for the various businesses now established within this building are collected by a not-for-profit company, RSA IV. The surpluses from these rents are transferred to the RSA Trust, a registered charity that manages the site and also funds local community start-ups and distributes grants in support of good causes.

The Enfield Island Village stands on the site of the former Royal Small Arms Factory (RSAF), the birthplace of the famous Lee–Enfield rifle. Prior to the opening of Enfield Island Village in 2001, it had been planned to open up the old barrel grinding mill headstream and barge turning circle that had remained, for many years, in-filled with rubble and concreted over. When the work was completed, a narrow boat was placed on the new water feature to make the connection between the small arms factory and the nearby Lee Navigation, which had been used for the transportation of goods and materials. Reeds were planted in the old barge turning circle and the pond soon became a haven for wildlife, attracting swans, mallards, moorhen and coots. Common birds like pied wagtails, blackbirds, finches and tits can be seen feeding around the pond's margins. In the summertime, dragonflies and damselflies dart and skim across their new artificially created pond.

The RSA Trust operates a small interpretation centre located under the nineteenth-century Italianate clock tower which was part of the old RSAF large machine room. Visitors wishing to view the centre's displays should enquire at the RSA Trust's on-site office about a fact-finding accompanied visit. Here we have a prime example of how a modern building development, on a former brown-field site, can be sensitively planned to take account of the history of the place while creating a scheme that is visually appealing to both residents and visitors and also an attraction to wildlife.

Rammey Marsh (Ordnance Road, Enfield, Middlesex EN3 6TH)

Entrance to this rough grassland site, which is intersected by a ditch from the Small River Lea, can be accessed from the Lee Navigation

(above) Bee orchid on Rammey Marsh Nature Reserve.

(above right) Pyramidal orchid on Rammey Marsh Nature Reserve.

towpath. The site ditch is connected to a seasonal pool, and both of these features support water voles and grass snakes. At the northern end of the site, in the months of May and June, a large colony of bee orchids form a glorious display that will not fail to please the visitor.

Rammey Marsh Nature Reserve.

Ponders End Lake (Lee Valley Golf Course, Meridian Way, Edmonton, London N6 0AR)

As the address might suggest, Ponders End Lake, which has a surface area of one acre, is a wildlife habitat in a rather unique setting. A path leads to a hide that can be accessed from a gate onto the golf course near the Lee Valley Leisure Complex. From this vantage point, look towards the reed-fringed areas of the lake to see reed and sedge warblers during the summer months and reed buntings all year round. Common terns, returning from their long flight from Africa, nest on the gravel surface of the lake's island.

Reed warbler at Ponders End Lake Nature Reserve.

Lapwings are often seen using the island and, in the winter, wigeon may be viewed on the lake and can be seen contentedly grazing on the golf course fairways. Kingfishers are occasionally known to flash by and can usually be distinguished from the flying golf ball by their bright ultramarine colour!

Chingford Reservoirs (Lea Valley Road, Chingford, London E4 7PX)

The Chingford Reservoirs are made up of the more northerly King George V and the William Girling. They are divided by the Lea Valley Road (A110), which is one of the few crossing points across the valley. Often, when driving or walking along this road, sheep can be seen grazing on the reservoir embankments, acting

A rare appearance by an unlikely visitor to the King George V Reservoir during the First World War. These were known as 'kites'.

as environmentally friendly lawnmowers. Interestingly, the William Girling is built on the site of the former Chingford Airfield, which was used to train Royal Navy Air Service (RNAS) flyers during the First World War. The reservoirs are owned by Thames Water and have been designated a site of special scientific interest (SSSI) due to their importance for over-wintering wildfowl. During the harsher months of the year, roosting gulls can number up to 50,000. These include species like common, herring, black-backed and black-headed.

Waterfowl which consist of teal, goosander and goldeneye over-winter on these reservoirs and the site is nationally recognised for wintering black-necked grebe. Rarer species of wildfowl can be brought into the area, particularly at times when harsh weather hits the European continent.

It is worth remembering that access to these reservoirs, because of deep water dangers, is not always possible, so it is worth contacting Thames Water to find out their current status before visiting.

Tottenham Marshes (Watermead Way, Tottenham, London N17 0XD)

The Lee Navigation crossing Tottenham Marshes.

Peregrine falcon on Tottenham Marshes.

Tottenham Marshes have changed out of all recognition since the 1950s. Once, dumped piles of cinder and clinker (the residue from industrial boiler furnaces) and other detritus littered the landscape, which also accommodated patches of bare soil, the tell-tale sign of a bicycle dirt track. On these compacted areas of earth, young boys, including the author, sped around madly on unsafe machines in pursuit of the new cycle speedway craze, trying to emulate their motorcycle heroes. Fortunately, through sensitive conservation and planting programmes, the marshes are now a large expanse of grassland with wildflower meadows where bee orchid numbers are annually increasing as well as the rarer wall bedstraw.

It is worth looking up near the top of the electricity pylons that cross the marsh as kestrels use these striding giants to perch while watching for movements of small mammals below. Sand martins have been encouraged to visit and nest on the marsh during the summer months. Holes drilled into the concrete wall culverting of Pymmes Brook provide the ideal home for these birds, the smallest of the swallow family, who have taken the long journey from Africa to reach the UK to breed. In winter, the marsh is also a good place

Stonechat on Tottenham Marshes.

to see many small birds, particularly linnets, which arrive to feed on seeds of teasel, dock and thistle.

Insects are doing well on the marsh, particularly the wasp spider, so called for its distinctive wasp-like markings. In recent years, their numbers have increased in Britain due mainly to improved summer temperatures. The species, originally an inhabitant of the Mediterranean, was first identified in the UK in the early 1920s in the warmer area of Britain's south coast. The marsh grassland provides the ideal habitat for this spider to lay its eggs and make its unique web, that has a characteristic zigzag pattern down the middle in which grasshoppers and small insects are trapped. Female spiders are around three times larger than the male and possess a nasty bite, which can make mating a little difficult for their partners, to say the least. During the mating process, it is not unusual for the male to end up bitten and wrapped in silk to provide a meal for the female – not a good start for any kind of relationship! The milder weather has encouraged the small red-eyed damselfly into the area. They can be seen in late June to September delicately balanced on floating vegetation on the nearby Lee Navigation.

Walthamstow Marshes (Lea Bridge Road, Leyton E10 7QL)

The Walthamstow Marshes are one of the few areas in the Lea Valley which can be claimed as Lammas Land and where the annual tradition of beating the bounds still takes place. Local people were

(above left) Walthamstow South Marsh in winter.

(above) Creeping marshwort on Walthamstow Marshes.

A rare Essex skipper on Walthamstow Marsh.

Belted Galloway grazing on Walthamstow Marsh.

once allowed to cut hay and graze their animals on these marshes. In 1981, the marshes were granted the status of a site of special scientific interest (SSSI). To maintain the unique grassland areas, the LVRPA introduced cattle to manage the marshes in the way it was traditionally done by local people. This will hopefully conserve the flora and fauna of the area for future generations to enjoy. It would appear that this plan is working as it has been recorded that the marshes support 350 different plant species. This includes the rare creeping marshwort with its tiny flowers, which can be seen along the grazed edges of draining ditches. Only on Walthamstow Marshes and on two other sites in the UK is this rare plant known to grow.

Seventeen species of butterfly breed on the marshes including the rare Essex skipper. In the summer, willow, sedge and reed warblers arrive to breed and join the indigenous reed bunting. Water voles colonise the drainage ditches and several species of small mammals populate the grassland areas, making the place an attractive hunting ground for kestrels.

In July 1909, the marsh provided the take-off site for Alliott Verdon Roe (of AVRO fame), who became the first Briton to fly in an all-British aircraft. His triplane (an aircraft with three wings) was constructed in two arches of the viaduct that carries the Liverpool Street to Chingford railway line across the Lee Navigation. A plaque on the viaduct wall commemorates the occasion.

Waterworks Nature Reserve (Lammas Road, off Lea Bridge Road, Leyton, London E10 7NU)

As the name suggests, this reserve has historic waterworks connections as it was built on the site of the former Essex Filter Beds that were part of the old Lea Bridge Waterworks complex. The site boasts one of the largest bird hides in London, where visitors can look out for a variety of wildfowl from the central hide, including gadwalls and shovelers. In the summer months, little grebes and pochards breed on site and winter is a good time to see teal and snipe. In spring and autumn, passing waders like common and green sandpipers regularly visit the site. Occasionally, the site has been known to attract rarer visitors such as black-tailed godwits and wood sandpipers.

Waterworks Nature Reserve.

Tufted duck at the Waterworks Nature Reserve.

In recent years, artificial nesting towers have been constructed for visiting sand martins, which the birds were originally grateful to call home. Each year the number of nesting pairs increased. However, in recent years the birds have not returned. The towers have been left in place just in case they change their minds. The towers are made out of large sections of concrete pipe drilled with holes around the perimeter and then stood vertically on end. An artificial nesting bank for kingfishers has also been constructed on site to see if these birds will take up the offer of an artificial home.

If you are an enthusiastic bird watcher, the Waterworks Nature Reserve is the place to go. From the seclusion of the hides, birds

Pochard at the Waterworks Nature Reserve.

like garden warblers, willow warblers, chiffchaffs, blackcaps, whitethroat, and sedge and reed warblers are amongst those that can be seen.

Middlesex Filter Beds (Lea Bridge Road, Leyton, London E5 9RB)

This reserve, a short distance from the Waterworks Nature Reserve, was constructed on the site of the former East London Waterworks Company (ELWC). The ELWC also built and owned the reservoirs off Ferry Lane which have now become the Walthamstow Wetlands nature reserve.

Of all the nature reserves within the Lee Valley Regional Park, the Middlesex Filter Beds are one of only a few that retain clues to their industrial past. Several of these clues have now been transformed into works of art. Those of us with an interest in industrial archaeology can marvel at the great granite blocks with their holes and grooves, now arranged as artwork around the reserve. These blocks were rescued from the site's old engine house when it was demolished and were probably the mountings for the massive iron flywheels and beam engines that were once used for pumping water. When the waterworks were built in the mid-nineteenth century, the Victorian engineers and scientists were desperately searching to find sources of cleaner water that were removed as far as possible from the contaminated supplies that had previously been taken from the River Thames.

View across the Middlesex Filter Beds Nature Reserve.

The reserve has a variety of habitats, which makes it a popular place for wildlife viewing throughout the year. Wooded areas attract flocks of finches and tits while the remains of industrial brickwork provide shelter for amphibians. In the spring, the wetland areas are home to toads, frogs and newts. Green and great spotted woodpeckers are often seen on site as well as sparrowhawks and kestrels that come in after hunting on the nearby Hackney Marsh. The waterway known as Middlesex Filter Beds Weir, which splits the

Middlesex Filter Beds Nature Reserve, constructed on the site of the former waterworks at Lea Bridge, Leyton.

Lee Navigation from the loop of the River Lea that flows across Hackney Marsh, is a good place to see grey wagtails and kingfishers, which nest along the river banks. Take a close look at the weir and an eel pass will be seen that allows eels to swim further up the River Lea. When the eels have matured, the eel pass allows them back to continue their long journey across the Atlantic to their traditional breeding ground in the Sargasso Sea, south of the Bahamas.

Over 200 plant species have been recorded growing on site, including purple loosestrife and cuckooflower, and several different mosses and liverworts have taken up residence along areas of old brickwork.

Bow Creek Ecology Park (Wharf Side Road, off Bidder Street, Canning Town, London E16 4ST)

Bow Creek Ecology Park, nestled in the meandering loop of Bow Creek, was once an osier bed where willow 'withies' were grown for making baskets, fish-traps, household furniture and also baby carriages (prams). Late-nineteenth-century maps show the site sitting adjacent to an industrial complex with several wharfs, a sack and bag works, an oil refinery, a galvanised-iron works and oil mills. This would have been an extremely unhealthy area to work and far removed from today's little East End wildlife haven that visitors can enjoy.

Bow Creek Ecology Park, a jewel in East London.

In summer, take the path through the wildflower meadow to see different species of butterfly that have been attracted to the nectar-producing plants. Orange tips, green-veined whites and small coppers are regularly seen. Between June and August, the magnificent emperor dragonflies emerge and at first both male and female are similarly coloured green, but later the male sports a sky-blue abdomen.

It is worth keeping a lookout over the tidal mudflats that surround the park as flocks of redshanks often take the opportunity to feed when the River Thames is on the ebb. Kestrel can be seen hunting along the verges of the Docklands Light Railway, which crosses the site. Reports of black redstarts in the area have been received by the LVRPA. These birds tend to favour habitats like derelict industrial sites.

Wildflowers grow at Bow Creek Ecology Park, where industry once prospered.

East India Dock Basin (Orchard Place, Canning Town, London E14 9QS)

As the name suggests, the dock was once the property of the East India Company, which built the docks in the early nineteenth century. From here East Indiamen sailed with goods to India and beyond for the East India Company and returned with cargoes of silk, tea and spices. During the Second World War, the dock was used to construct the floating Mulberry Harbours that were successfully used in the 1944 D-Day Landings in France.

The Dock Basin was once served by giant lock gates which, when closed, protected the penned-in water from being lowered by the falling tide on the River Thames. This allowed ships to be loaded or unloaded while being kept afloat.

Now the Dock Basin, with its brackish water, acts as a tidal lagoon and is one of the more unusual London nature reserves. At the northern end, there are mudflats with a small salt-marsh area

East India Dock Basin gates.

supporting common reed, sea club-rush, buttonweed, sea milkwort, sea arrowgrass and wild celery. The grassland area supports many native flowers including lady's bedstraw and also some other interesting plants like salsify and warty cabbage.

Every summer, a colony of common terns returns to the artificial rafts on the lagoon. Cormorants can also be seen throughout the year in characteristic pose with wings open and half-folded, catching the early sun. In the winter months, large numbers of shelducks and flocks of over 150 teal can be seen. Black redstarts often visit

Urban habitats, East India Dock Basin.

Urban habitats, East India Dock Basin.

the site, especially in spring and autumn. In the bordering scrub, a barred warbler was recently recorded.

It is worth taking binoculars as the site provides a good vantage point to look across the River Thames towards the O2 Arena. Peregrine falcons and a wide variety of gulls can be seen, on a good day, in the area of the O2 Arena's support towers.

Common teal at the East India Dock Basin Nature Reserve.

References

Author unknown, *Where to Watch Wildlife in the Lee Valley*, Lee Valley Regional Park Authority, 2012

Bromberg, Stephen, Head of Communications, LVRPA, personal conversation, December 2016

Lewis, Jim, *London's Lea Valley: Britain's Best Kept Secret*, Phillimore & Co. Ltd., Chichester, 1999

Lewis, Jim, *London's Lea Valley: More Secrets Revealed*, Phillimore & Co. Ltd., Chichester, 2001

Patrick, Cath, Senior Conservation Officer, LVRPA, personal conversation, December 2016

Notes

All images used in this chapter have been provided by:

Lee Valley Regional Park Authority

Hertfordshire & Middlesex Wildlife Trust

Brenda Chanter

Brian Anderson

Dennis Meadhurst

Graham Canny

Ken Bentley

Mark Braun

Paul Lister

Steven Swaby

Tim Hill

At the end of this book, a number of blank pages have been left to allow the traveller to make their own notes about places of particular interest on their journey along the Lee Navigation.

www.ingramcontent.com/pod-product-compliance
Lightning Source LLC
Chambersburg PA
CBHW051317110526
44590CB00031B/4389